# THE HISTORY OF CHINA

*A Concise Introduction to Chinese History, Culture, Dynasties, Mythology, Great Achievements & More of The Oldest Living Civilization*

HISTORY BROUGHT ALIVE

## © Copyright 2022 - All rights reserved.

The content contained within this book may not be reproduced, duplicated, or transmitted without direct written permission from the author or the publisher.

Under no circumstances will any blame or legal responsibility be held against the publisher, or author, for any damages, reparation, or monetary loss due to the information contained within this book, either directly or indirectly.

Legal Notice:

This book is copyright protected. It is only for personal use. You cannot amend, distribute, sell, use, quote, or paraphrase any part, or the content within this book, without the consent of the author or publisher.

Disclaimer Notice:

Please note the information contained within this document is for educational and entertainment purposes only. All effort has been executed to present accurate, up-to-date, reliable, complete information. No warranties of any kind are declared or implied. Readers acknowledge that the author is not engaged in the rendering of legal, financial, medical, or professional advice. The content within this book has been derived from various sources. Please consult a licensed professional before attempting any techniques outlined in this book.

By reading this document, the reader agrees that under no circumstances is the author responsible for any losses, direct or indirect, that are incurred as a result of the use of the information contained within this document, including, but not limited to, errors, omissions, or inaccuracies.

# FREE BONUS FROM HBA: EBOOK BUNDLE

Greetings!

First of all, thank you for reading our books. As fellow passionate readers of History and Mythology, we aim to create the very best books for our readers.

Now, we invite you to join our VIP list. As a welcome gift, we offer the History & Mythology Ebook Bundle below for free. Plus you can be the first to receive new books and exclusives! <u>Remember it's 100% free to join.</u>

Simply click the link below to join.

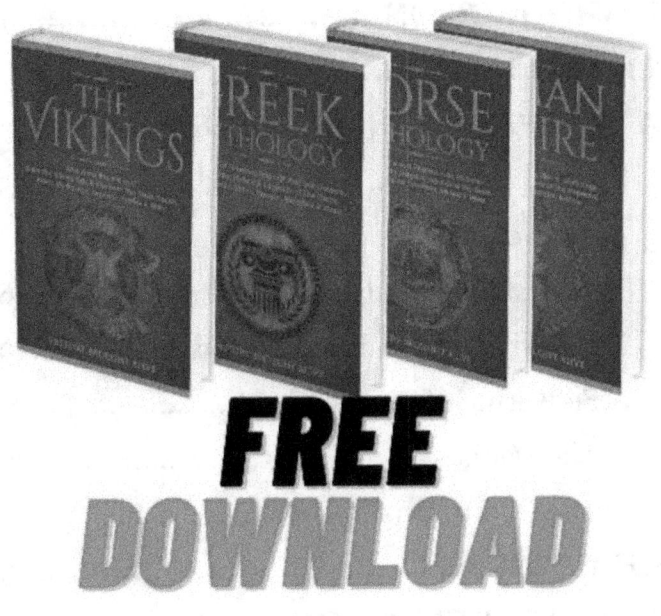

### Keep up to date with us on:

YouTube: History Brought Alive

Facebook: History Brought Alive

www.historybroughtalive.com

# CONTENTS

**INTRODUCTION** ............................................. 1
**CHAPTER 1** ................................................... 9
***A TIME OF MYTH AND LEGEND*** ......... 9
    Geography .......................................................... 13
    Archeology .......................................................... 14
    The First Kingdoms ........................................ 16
    The Spring and Autumn Period ................... 19
    A Flowering of Philosophy ............................ 21
        The Daoists ................................................ 22
        The Confucians ......................................... 23
**CHAPTER 2** ................................................. 25
***THE FIRST EMPEROR*** ........................ 25
    The Warring States ......................................... 26
    Qin Shi Huang Di ............................................. 28
    The Qin Empire ................................................ 30
    The Han Empire ............................................... 33
**CHAPTER 3** ................................................. 37
***A UNIFIED CIVILIZATION FRAGMENTS***
.......................................................................... 37
    The Romance of the Three Kingdoms ........ 39

    The Western Jin .............................................. 43

    Fragmentation and Conflict......................... 43

    The Sui Empire................................................ 46

**CHAPTER 4 ......................................... 49**

***ENTER A GOLDEN AGE ...................... 49***

    Founding of the Tang .................................... 51

    Early Achievements....................................... 52

    The Reign of Empress Wu ............................ 57

    Late Achievements ........................................ 60

**CHAPTER 5 ......................................... 63**

***A DYNASTY BESET BY ENEMIES ....... 63***

    Establishment................................................. 64

    Hostile Neighbors .......................................... 66

    Northern and Southern Song....................... 69

    The Mongol Terror ........................................ 74

**CHAPTER 6 ......................................... 78**

***THE MONGOLS RULE CHINA ............ 78***

    Marco Polo...................................................... 80

    Kublai's China ................................................ 82

    Victory and Consolidation ........................... 87

    Quest for Expansion...................................... 90

**CHAPTER 7 ......................................... 94**

## THE MIGHTY MING .......................... 94
- Red Turbans and White Lotus..................... 96
- China Ascendant ........................................... 101
- An Age of Exploration.................................102
- Decline Into Crisis........................................104

## CHAPTER 8 ...................................... 107
## THE MAGNIFICENT QING................. 107
- The Rise of the Manchus ............................109
- The Beneficent Reign of Kangxi ................. 111
- The Glorious Reign of Qianlong................. 115
- Encroaching Enemies ................................. 118

## CHAPTER 9 ...................................... 129
## REVOLUTION AND WORLD WAR .... 129
- Sun Yat-Sen and the Revolution ................ 131
- Chang Kai-Shek's China ............................136
- The Long March of the Communists..........139
- Japan Invades ..............................................144
- Civil War Resumes ......................................145

## CHAPTER 10...................................... 147
## THE PEOPLE'S REPUBLIC OF CHINA ........................................................... 147
- Taking The Great Leap Forward ................149
- The Cultural Revolution .............................156

An Era of Modernization ............................ 161

China Transforms.........................................164

**CONCLUSION** .....................................**172**

Ancient China (pre-221 BCE).................. 173

The First Imperial Age (221 BCE to 580 CE) ...............................................................174

The Second Imperial Age (581 CE to 1270 CE)...........................................................175

The Third Imperial Age (1271 CE to 1911 CE)...........................................................175

The Modern Age (1912 CE to present)...176

**PRONUNCIATION GUIDE** ..................**181**

**TIMELINE**........................................... **183**

**END NOTE** ......................................... **185**

**REFERENCES** .................................... **186**

**OTHER BOOKS BY HISTORY BROUGHT ALIVE** ................................................ **195**

**FREE BONUS FROM HBA: EBOOK BUNDLE** ............................................ **198**

# INTRODUCTION

China is one of the world's great civilizations. Unlike other comparable civilizations of bygone eras, such as those in ancient Egypt, Mesopotamia, or the Indus Valley, China's civilization is not only ancient but continuous. Whereas the monuments of other great civilizations now lie in ruins; their people scattered or colonized by newcomers, and their languages dead or forgotten; the language, culture, and people of China have endured, persisting through the millennia until this very day. For this reason, **China represents the world's oldest living civilization**.


Astonishingly, for over 2000 of the past 5000 years of recorded human history, the achievements of Chinese civilization are beyond compare. In that time, China led the world in astronomy, chemistry, medicine, agriculture, metallurgy, the arts, and the art of war. It had the biggest population, the wealthiest treasury, the greatest fleets, the most advanced technology, the strongest military, and the largest effectively planned cities. China was not only at the center of world trade, but it was also the center of tribute for foreign nations who could not hope to compare with its power.


Despite this rarified status in world history, public knowledge of history of China is sorely lacking. Many people in western cultures can name more than one Roman Emperor, but how many can name a Chinese Emperor? We argue that the Emperors of China are of equal significance. It is for this reason that [History Brought Alive](#) brings you this concise, comprehensive, and accurate history of China.

You may have already tried to learn about Chinese history and have found it to be an unpleasant task. Most currently available books on the topic are unwieldy, written in lengthy and dense academic prose. Few cover the entire sweep of Chinese history in chronological order, and, due to China's position as the last remaining communist-governed world power, some authors present a bias towards or against its political ideology. Should learning about this awe-inspiring civilization be uncomfortable and uninteresting? Absolutely not—this is the book for you!

Together, we will journey through Chinese history in an immersive and engaging manner, while revealing its fascinating humanity and epic grandeur. Beginning from the earliest creation myths and the first archeological evidence of complex societies, we will ground your understanding in the foundations of China's past. The all-important geographical context of these fledgling societies will then be discussed. Once the reader is familiar with the Yellow River Basin and these deep roots of Chinese culture, we will progress sequentially through the five eras of Chinese history: Ancient China, the First Imperial Age, the Second Imperial Age, the Third Imperial Age, and the Modern Age.

At each step of the journey, we will be confronted by the trials and tribulations faced by the Chinese people. These may be external challenges, such as foreign invaders or rival nations, or internal challenges, such as natural disasters or social rebellions. The remarkable responses of the Chinese people in the face of these difficulties will be discussed innovations in governance, education, agriculture, technology, and military organization. A cast of exceptional characters will be introduced as we move through time—some heroic, some villainous, some tragic—enabling us to personally identify with the highs and lows experienced by this epic civilization.

As you read, you will discover a social philosophy that has spread across East Asia, and a unique indigenous religion practiced by millions. You will be confronted by great leaders and their incredible military campaigns. World firsts, including inventions important to global histories, such as paper money, insurance, and the moveable-type printing press, will be introduced. The shattering effect of 20th-century history and China's place in World War II will be explored in-depth, and we will end with a discussion of the rise of the contemporary People's Republic of China.

By the conclusion of the journey, the reader will be well-versed with Chinese culture and the unique circumstances and character of its people. The concise nature of the book is expanded upon by a list of authoritative references for those who wish to dive deeper into over 6000 years of drama and intrigue. Written without political bias, this book will enable you to interact more effectively with people from China—a most important goal in this globalized age.

We at **History Brought Alive** pride ourselves on producing expertly crafted works that enrich the reader and provide new insights into the past. Our existing titles include books on Roman history, Greek mythology, Norse mythology, Ancient Egyptian history, among many more.

Well-written, thoroughly researched, and comprehensive, this history of China is yet another must-have on your shelf from **History Brought Alive**.


China in 2021 represents the world's second-largest economy and the world's biggest manufacturer. In today's globalized world, we are all linked in some way to China. If you wear clothes from brands like Adidas or Prada, if you own electronics made by giants such as Apple or Dell, or if you drive a Volkswagen or a Honda, you are in a trading relationship with China. Professionally, you may have Chinese colleagues or interact with Chinese clients. Your company may even be Chinese owned! This book is therefore indispensable, not only for students of history but for all of us making our way in the contemporary world.


Learning about China in the 21st century is

critically important. Read on, to discover the remarkable history of China. This book presents an immersive, engaging, and exciting journey into China's past—a story of vast geographic scope, encompassing over ten thousand years of archeological history and involving the lives of billions of people.

This is how history should be told: **History Brought Alive**.

# CHAPTER 1
## *A TIME OF MYTH AND LEGEND*

How did the world begin? Every culture and civilization have its own legends. The Chinese creation myth, unlike those of western cultures, begins not with a first cause, but with a Great Void:

In the beginning, there was nothing. No time, no space, no phenomena, no appearance. Only a cosmic void pregnant with potential. Within the potential of this void, an egg grew. Within the egg there appeared the positive force of yang and the negative force of yin. A hairy, horned giant, the first being, grew within this egg. His name was Pangu. With a roar, he cleaved the forces of yin and yang apart and broke the cosmic egg.

Pangu pushed yang upwards to become the sky and trod yin beneath him so that it became the earth. He grew in size and might, separating earth and sky far apart until eventually his work was done. Satisfied, he died. As he died, his body transformed. His blood became the rivers; his sweat the rain; his breath the wind; and his voice, thunder. Pangu's limbs became the earth and his torso the mountains, his hair, and beard the stars and planets. The moon was his right eye, and his left eye, the sun. The world was formed from Pangu (Keay, 2009).

Millions of years passed, and many divine beings emerged within the world. Fuxi and Nuwa were twin beings, both brother-sister, and husband-wife. Nuwa sculpted figures from the yellow clay of the great river and gave them life—these living clay figures were the first human beings. Fuxi tamed animals, studied the heavens, and through his marriage to Nuwa, instituted the family.

The next great being who emerged was Shennong. Shennong gave humanity the gift of agriculture, the knowledge of digging wells, and the practice of herbal medicine. His successor was known as the Yellow Emperor. The Yellow Emperor taught humanity the use of weaponry and led the tribes of the Yellow River to victory in their first-ever battle; the battle of Banquan.

These divine culture heroes created the basis of Chinese civilization—a feudal military civilization with knowledge of agriculture and medicine, based on the institution of the family. On the banks of the Yellow River, this civilization prospered and grew until disaster struck. The river itself, the giver of life, became the enemy, flooding uncontrollably and destroying everything in its path.

It was at this time that a new hero emerged; the Yellow Emperor's great-great-grandson: Yu. Yu rebelled against the water-control management practices of the time—instead of damming rivers, he dredged them; instead of reinforcing riverbanks, he dug overflow channels to carry excess water into the fields. His approach was an incredible success, and the raging river was tamed. Indebted, the King of the time offered him the throne, and Yu the Great became the founder of the Xia Dynasty (Wright, 2011).

## Geography

These are China's foundational myths and legends, but what about the objective truth? The story of China begins with the stories of two things: the story of a people, the ethnic Han, and the story of a river, the Huang Ho, or the Yellow River.

The Yellow River rises high in the Tibetan Plateau, over four thousand meters above sea level, and over five thousand kilometers from the sea. In its upper course, it runs swift and crystal clear across the high plateau, before plunging through a series of gorges and cataracts. Down it falls until it spreads onto the Loess Plateau. Here the river turns north, then east, then south, tracing a great loop across north-central China. Particulate matter blown in from the deserts and steppes to the north and west compose the loess plateau; in places, this sediment is tens to hundreds of meters thick.

The river erodes this fertile soil, becoming heavy with the yellow silt that provides it with its name. On completion of its great loop, the river turns east, spreading out across the north China plain on its way to the sea. Here the river brings the gift and curse of the Loess—the fertility and the sedimentation of the silt. As the silt settles on the riverbed, it gradually raises the river to the level of the surrounding land. When spring floods come, the river is liable to burst its banks, or even change course completely, wreaking death and destruction across the land (Wright, 2011).

## Archeology

Modern visitors to China may be surprised to find that it is a country of 56 official ethnic groups and 302 recognized languages. In ancient times China was even more ethnically and culturally diverse. But the story of China is, to a large extent, the story of the prosperity and rise to dominance of a people known as the ethnic Han. The ethnic Han makes up the majority of the 1.4 billion population of contemporary China, and the majority of the 50 million people of the modern Chinese diaspora. Genetic evidence ties the modern Han Chinese population to the peoples of the Yellow River who lived three thousand years ago (Zhao et al, 2015).

Archeological evidence reveals that the lives of the hunter-gatherer tribes who lived by the Yellow River began to transform around 8000 BCE with the domestication of the cereal crop millet. Four thousand years later, wet rice cropping was introduced from the south, enabling plentiful harvests. The secret of silk soon followed—a secret the Chinese were to the harbor for millennia—and then metallurgy developed. By 2700 BCE, the tribes of the Yellow River knew how to work jade and many of the basic elements of what we now know as

Chinese culture were in place.

Remarkably, the fanciful legends of divine beings parallel the development of Chinese civilization. Fuxi and Nuwa could be thought of as representing the tribal era; Shennong, the agricultural; and the Yellow Emperor an organized military state possessing the ability to work metals and jade (Ferguson & Masaharu, 1928). But what of Yu the Great and his mastery of the waters? Incredibly, there is archeological evidence of a period of catastrophic flooding of the Yellow River beginning 1920 BCE, with a renewal of cultural development following in its wake (Wu et al, 2016).

## The First Kingdoms

The culture arising in the wake of the great flood of 1920 BCE may have been the Xia dynasty, however, without written evidence, archeologists are reluctant to apply a definitive label. The first dynasty of China according to written evidence is the Shang dynasty, which was founded in 1600 BCE. We know of the Shang dynasty because their earliest writing, taking the form of pictographs scratched into bone, is the direct predecessor of the modern Chinese script (Wright, 2011). The artful, stylized calligraphy that we recognize as the written Chinese of today is a descendant of the Shang practice of drawing pictures to represent things and ideas.

Shang society was one of the aristocrats served by shaman-priests, who ruled over commoners and slaves. Two of the classic features of Chinese religious life were already in place at this time: the worship of ancestors, and the practice of divination (the earliest writing was found on burnt bones that had been used as oracles) (Cao & Sun, 2011). Bronze working was refined to a high level of sophistication, and bronze ware decorated palaces and equipped their formidable military.

The Shang dynasty lasted for an astonishing 600 years. Later writings, which cannot be regarded as a reliable, state that the late Kings of the dynasty became tyrannical. An aristocratic rebellion led to a civil war which was won by a man named Fa Ji, who became King Wu, founder of the Zhou Dynasty. His brother, known as the Duke of Wu, assisted in strengthening and consolidating the newly won kingdom. As the Shang were a society that practiced divination and so claimed to be a kingship guided by the divine, the Duke of Wu introduced a counterclaim to legitimize the new dynasty. The Duke explained that the **Mandate of Heaven**, the will of the divine, existed to ensure a just ruler. If the rulers were unjust, as the Shang were believed to be, then Heaven would see to it that a new, better, and more just, the dynasty would arise to take their place (Kerr, 2013).

## The Spring and Autumn Period

The Zhou kingship continued in slow decline for three hundred years, as the power of its feudal vassals grew. Eventually, in 771 BCE, one of the vassals, the Marquess of Shen, allied with nomadic tribes and sacked the capital. King You of Zhou was killed, and the court fled east from their heartland on the Wei River, establishing a new capital city downstream on the lower Yellow River.

So begins the timeline of what is known as the Eastern Zhou Dynasty. A classic of Chinese literature written during this period, *The Spring and Autumn Annals*, gives its name to the first three hundred years of the Eastern Zhou. The Zhou system was a network of production and distribution controlled by feudal landowners, with their vassalage centralized around the king. Commoners were obligated to complete work in their feudal master's fields before time was allotted to tend their personal plots. The produce of these feudal fields was presented as a tribute to the King, who in turn rationed it to the populace as necessary. The practice of gift-giving circulated luxuries amongst the upper classes.

With the move of the Zhou court eastward, this

system began to break down. New iron tools and ox-driven plowing techniques vastly improved the efficiency of agricultural labor. Workers began to resent the time spent on forced labor, and landowners were driven to lease out the communal land in exchange for rent that they kept, rather than presented to the King. This process of the privatization of land and property accelerated, in turn driving demand for the products of artisans and stimulating long-distance trade. By the end of the Spring and Autumn period, coins were being minted and a vibrant market economy had taken root. In this time of incredible change, some feudal lords became destitute while others prospered, and the common person was enabled to develop and financially benefit from his or her individual talents (Zhang, 2015).

## A Flowering of Philosophy

The development of the market economy was

able to support a new class of individuals. These were the scholars, who, thanks to long-distance trading, could now move more freely across the land, and, no longer restricted by clan boundaries, they were able to discuss and exchange ideas. This was the beginning of the *"one hundred schools of thought"*—the incipient intellectual sphere of the Chinese cultural world. Two of these schools would go on to become major pillars in the foundations of Chinese culture; the Confucians, and the Daoists.

## *The Daoists*

The major text of the Daoists, the Dao de Jing, was written by Laozi. In legend, he was considered to be a royal record keeper in the court of the Eastern Zhou. Long-lived and wise, he eventually tired of the corruption of civic and royal life and retreated from society into the mountains. Before he left forever, he compiled his teaching into the Dao de Jing.

In this work, he describes the birth of the Cosmos and outlines the path of living a life in harmony with the workings of the Cosmos, which he named the Dao or the Way. His teaching, known as Daoism, was to become the predominant indigenous religion of China, and its philosophy informed the entirety of Chinese thought that followed (Cao & Sun, 2011).

## *The Confucians*

Confucius (also known as Kongzi), whose existence has much more historical veracity than that of Laozi, was considered as a younger contemporary of the latter. Whereas Laozi counseled a retreat from society and a return to nature, Confucius was concerned with the problem of how to live an effective life within society. He created the idea of a moral society based on benevolent goodwill to all people and deference to authority. In Confucianism, the ideal of the moral man, who knew his place within the social order, and who strived for perfection through self-cultivation was established. The records of his teachings, *The Analects*, would go on to provide not only the ethical foundation of Chinese culture, but also the ethical foundation of Japanese, Korean, and Vietnamese society (Wright, 2011).

This "Spring and Autumn" era of the Eastern Zhou lasted from 771 BCE to 476 BCE. During this time, the influence of the Eastern Zhou kings steadily waned as their feudal vassals expanded their territory and exerted their autonomy. Gradually, the hundreds of petty fiefdoms supposedly subservient to the Zhou king consolidated, either through warfare or by the alliance. With the partition of the state of Jin in 453 BCE, only seven states remained, and the stage was set for conflict. Which of the seven states would be able to reign supreme?

# CHAPTER 2
## *THE FIRST EMPEROR*

---

March 1974. Six brothers were digging a well in a field near the city of Xian. They dug steadily downward; down through the changing shades of different layers of earth, until, with a *clang*, their spades hit something hard. One of the brothers pulled up the obstruction—it was a piece of terracotta.

How strange, they thought.

As they worked, they scooped up more and more fragments of terracotta, bricks made of terracotta, and small pieces of bronze. Little did they know that they had discovered bronze arrowheads, the brick foundations of an enclosure, and pieces of an army of life-sized terracotta warriors—an army built to guard the resting place of the First Emperor of China (Wright, 2011).

## The Warring States

Yan, Qi, Wei, Chu, Zhou, Han, and Qin were the names of the seven states that occupied the heartland of China at the tail end of the Eastern Zhou dynasty; a heartland that had grown from its historic center on the eastwards bend of the Yellow River to also encapsulate the lower reaches of the second great river of China, the Chiang Jiang (known to the west as the Yangtze). These two mighty rivers, and their surrounding floodplains and highlands, would be the field where the battle for control of China would play out.

At the outset of hostilities, Qin was one of the smaller states vying for domination, and in the early years of the period, it played a marginal role in the wars and intrigues of the time. Qin's placement of the western margins of Chinese civilization, however, gave it a geographical advantage: the state's location on the banks of the Wei River meant that it was protected by mountains to its north, south, and west. It only had to worry about the invasion from the east.

The Qin leadership made wise use of their circumstances. In 361 BCE, they appointed Shang Yang, a luminary of one of the thousand schools of thought, to the position of the chief minister. Shang Yan was not a Confucian or a Daoist, he was a Legalist, who believed in absolute law enforced by absolute power. His vision was of a society centralized under an absolute ruler, and he believed that the purpose of every individual person was to work tirelessly in support of this society. Shan Yang used his new office to put his theory into practice, reducing the power of the Qin aristocracy and centralizing the military under the King of Qin. Forced labor became the task of the common people, with only the most productive able to take on other roles. The State of Qin was honed into a singular instrument of war (Zhang, 2011).

## Qin Shi Huang Di

Thanks to Shang Yang's influence, the power of the Qin state steadily grew. Qin annexed the plains of the Sichuan Basin to the southwest, and, through a revolutionary system of irrigation and flood control, increased their fertility. The other states of China recognized Qin's rising menace and sought to check its power. Some court intellectuals, drawn from the ranks of the one hundred schools of thought, counseled a "vertical alliance" whereby Yan, Qi, Wei, Chou, Zhou, and Han would join forces to make a power block that was capable of resisting or even defeating the Qin. An alternative school of thought was the "horizontal alliance," which promoted the idea of a state allying itself to Qin in order to break this deadlock. This state would then support Qin's rise to dominance as a partner in power.

In the year 247 BCE, a new king inherited the throne of Qin. Ying Zheng, only 13-years-old at the time of his ascension, would go on to distinguish himself as a remarkable leader and a cunning tactician. By 235 BCE, he had rid the Qin court of all rivals and, by 230 BCE, he had formulated a strategy to conquer all of China; he would ally with the states most distant from Qin, and attack the states nearest to Qin. In this way, he would encourage the ambitions of those states wishing to form a "horizontal alliance" and undermine the threat of any "vertical alliance" against him.

The bordering kingdom of Han was the first state to fall. Qin then took advantage of natural disasters to invade Zhou. Wei was conquered after whole rivers were diverted to flood its capital. Chu was next to be vanquished, followed by Yan. Qi, the last remaining state and "ally" to Qin, surrendered in order to save its people from the massacre. Ying Zheng had conquered all of the lands of the former Zhou dynasty, and he bestowed upon himself a new title: "Qin Shi Huang Di". Echoing the legend of "Huang Di" or the Yellow Emperor, he had named himself *The First Emperor of the Qin Dynasty* (Cao & Sun, 2011).

## The Qin Empire

Qin Shi Huang Di's military campaigns did not cease with the defeat of the Qi state. He sent his generals south, where they conquered the regions of southern China that were not ethnically Han, and to the northeast, where they defeated the nomadic tribes that had, for millennia, menaced the frontiers of Chinese civilization. To prevent the re-incursion of the nomads, the Emperor ordered the building of a rammed earth barrier across the northern frontier; this would form part of the foundation of the later Great Wall of China.

The new Emperor now turned his attention to statecraft, and together with his brilliant minister Li Si, another Legalist in the tradition of Shang Yang, Qin Shi Huang Di set about transforming China into a singular state under his supreme rule. The feudal system that had, for centuries, provided the structure of Chinese civilization was abolished in a single stroke. The state became the sole owner of the land, and a system of civil administration was created to administer public works and to manage taxation. This hierarchical structure, unlike the hereditary land ownership that preceded it, was appointed through ability and merit. Chinese script was standardized, as were the weights and measures used at markets, and a new currency was minted.

Great public works were enacted, including new roads and canals, and a countrywide census informed the leadership of every detail of the land and people. Political thought was strictly controlled, and in a famous incident over which

Li Si presided, the Confucian classics were burned and the scholars who did not denounce these works were buried alive. Within a generation, the Warring States had been transformed into a singular Empire. When Qin Shi Huang Di died in his eleventh year of rule, he was buried in a mausoleum the size of a city. Eternally guarded by an army of life-sized terracotta soldiers that would watch over his grave remained undisturbed, and unrecorded by history, until that fateful digging of a well in the spring of 1974 (Wright, 2011).

## The Han Empire

Qin Shi Huang Di's new empire did not last long. His heirs became puppets of court intrigue, and the harsh punishments of the Empire's Legalist regime began to antagonize the populace. A two-faction rebellion broke out, with both led by army deserters, and, after five years of war, the Qin Empire was overthrown.

Emperor Gaozu of the Han dynasty took his seat of authority. Emperor Gaozu threw himself into the task of revitalizing the Empire. To the generals that had accompanied him to victory, he gifted kingdoms, partially recreating the feudal system, but he also maintained Qin Shi Huang Di's merit-based system of officialdom. The tax burden on the populace was reduced, and the growth of families was encouraged by exempting new parents from forced labor. Agricultural production was prioritized.

Gaozu's example of the rule in service to the people was followed by his successors, and by the time of the fifth Emperor of the Han, Emperor Wu, China was prospering as it never had before. The Han's focus on agriculture had massively boosted production, which, in turn, had stimulated commerce. Subsequently, commerce encouraged innovation, and Chinese society progressed in astonishing ways. Inventions of this time included paper, the seed drill, the wrought iron manufacturing process, and ocean-going sea vessels (Kerr, 2013).

In the intellectual sphere, there were advances in the fields of astronomy, geology, mathematics, and medicine. Politically, Emperor Wu broke the association of Chinese Emperors with Legalism and enshrined Confucianism as the official court doctrine; inaugurating a position it would hold for more than two millennia. The Confucian classics that had been purged under Qin Shi Huang Di were once again recorded as the Chinese cultural tradition of oral history had saved them for posterity.

Under Emperor Wu, China became strong enough to send punitive military missions out to confront the steppe tribes that continually threatened its borders. The Xiongnu, a major nomad confederacy, were defeated, and China gained control of vast new regions in the northwest. China now directly bordered the cultures of central Asia, and this connection initiated the Silk Road trade route (Cao & Sun, 2011). The years from 202 BCE to 189 CE were considered to be a golden age. So esteemed in fact, that the ethnic Chinese to this day use the name of this dynasty to refer to themselves: the Han.

# CHAPTER 3
## *A UNIFIED CIVILIZATION FRAGMENTS*

Visitors to any Chinatown (a common name for neighborhoods with a majority Chinese population) in the world today will no doubt cross paths with a statue of a fearsome warrior. Clad in magnificent robes over metallic armor, he brandishes a fearsome polearm in one hand. Most curiously, his skin is a deep, coppery red, and his eyebrows are large, bushy, and black. His long, black beard flows down across his breast, and he carries an air of authority and regal grandeur.

This hallowed ancestral figure is the image of a man real to history; he is Guan Yu, one of the heroes mythologized in the Chinese classic *Romance of the Three Kingdoms*. The classic was written in the 14th century, during the Yuan Dynasty, but the events of the book are from an earlier era. Guan Yu was a blood-brother of Liu

Bei, and he distinguished himself as a paragon of loyalty and martial virtue during the period's incessant conflict, until his untimely death at the hands of Liu Bei's erstwhile ally, Sun Quan.

# The Romance of the Three Kingdoms

The beneficent reign of the first five Emperors of the Han was not to last. Problems were growing at the bottom, middle, and top of society. The well-being of the peasant farmer, so important to the establishment and prosperity of the Empire, was neglected as taxes rose, causing mass impoverishment. As a consequence, Daoist protest movements, including the *Yellow Turbans* and the *Five Pecks of Rice*, gained popularity amongst the common people. These movements preached that the Emperor had lost the Mandate of Heaven and so rebellion and overthrow of the imperial order were justified (Keay, 2009).

As central control broke down, the fiefdoms grew in power and began to absorb one another. By the year 207 CE, three warlords had established themselves as China's leading military powers and they were on a collision course: Cao Cao, Sun Quan, and Liu Bei. Of the three, Cao Cao was closest to the imperial regime—he was a brilliant statesman who served as Minister of Works under the Emperor. Tasked with quelling revolt and banditry, he used his powers to expand his sphere of influence from within the center of the floundering Han empire. Sun Quan was the son of an official, while Liu Bei was born into poverty. Both had distinguished themselves as supporters of the government, Sun Quan by his military activities against the hill tribes of the south, and Liu Bei by his leading of militias against the Yellow Turbans.

Cao Cao held the upper hand in the conflict, as the court of the Emperor was under his military oversight, and his forces controlled the heartland of China. Victory after victory followed in Cao Cao's campaigns until he was in a position to invade the south of China. A late alliance between Liu Bei and Sun Quan met Cao Cao's superior forces on the banks of the Red Cliffs of the Yangtze. Through brilliant tactics involving fire ships and a surprise marine assault, Liu Bei and Sun Quan were able to defeat Cao Cao's overwhelming army and navy (Zhang, 2015).

Cao Cao retreated to the north, and Sun Quan married his sister Liu Bei to cement their alliance. China had essentially been divided into three. Twelve years after the Battle of the Red Cliffs, Cao Cao's son Cao Pi forced the last of the Han imperial leaders, Emperor Xian, to abdicate, and declared himself the first Emperor of the Wei dynasty. In response, Liu Bei proclaimed himself as Emperor of the Shu dynasty, and Sun Quan named himself the King of Wu (later, he would declare himself Emperor Wu).

These three Empires would remain locked in antagonism until Wei was able to conquer Shu in 263 CE. Before Wei could turn its attention to the state of Wu, however, the dynasty was usurped from within. With echoes of Cao Pi's deposition of the Han Emperor, Sima Yan, head of the powerful Sima clan, forced the abdication of Cao Huan, grandson of Cao Cao, and assumed the title of Emperor of the Jin Dynasty. By 279 CE the Jin Empire had the resources to launch a massive offensive against the state of Wu. Five armies invaded southern China across the Yangtze, in tandem with an armada that swept down the coastline. It was an onslaught that Wu could not withstand and, within months, their Emperor had surrendered (Kerr, 2013). China was unified once more.

## The Western Jin

Only thirty years after its founding, Western Jin found itself in a state of crisis. The imperial successor, Emperor Hui, suffered from an inherited disability and, consequently, a power struggle broke out amongst his extended family as they sought for de facto control of the throne. The warring factions of the Sima family hired mercenaries from the ethnicities that fringed the Chinese world; the Xiongnu, the Jie, the Di, the Qiang, and the Xianbei (Zhang, 2015). Sima Yue emerged victorious from the family struggle, but his victory was won at the cost of a state in crisis.

## Fragmentation and Conflict

The peoples who fringed the lands of China, and who populated its highlands and hinterlands, were considered by the ethnic Han to be "barbarians". They were the yardstick by which the ethnic Han measured their own civilizational progress. But in the year 304 CE, the barbarians would achieve their revenge.

Recognizing the weakness of the Jin state, armies led by these tribespeople began to run amok in northern China. In 311 CE, an army led by members of the Xiongnu tribe captured the Jin capital of Luoyang and razed it to the ground, massacring the entire populace and despoiling the graves of the imperial ancestors. Emperor Huai of Jin was killed, but members of his court and family were able to flee, eventually founding a new capital near modern-day Nanjing. This marked the beginning of the Eastern Jin dynasty. Eastern Jin still controlled all of China south of the Yangtze, but to the north and west civilization was in a state of near collapse as the Jie, the Di, the Qiang, and the Xianbei flooded in to join the Xiongnu in declaring their own kingdoms over the ruins of the Jin state (Keay, 2009).

For over one hundred years, wars raged amongst these petty feudal domains of the north, in an era known to posterity as the "Sixteen Kingdoms". The south was not altogether stable too, as the Jin Empire was usurped by the Liu Song Dynasty. Remarkably, this period of chaos did not extinguish the spirit of Chinese culture. The ruling class of the "barbarians" of the north adopted many aspects of Chinese culture, and the mass migration of ethnic-Han into the south led to the region outstripping the north in terms of productivity and technical knowledge for the first time in history (Cao & Sun, 2011). In the north, the new religion of Buddhism, first introduced during the Han dynasty, continued to spread, as did the teachings of Daoism (Kerr, 2013).

Gradually, the north was unified under the Wei

dynasty, while the leadership of the south passed from the Liu Song Dynasty to the Southern Qi, then Liang, and finally the Chen. The Wei dynasty fractured into the Northern Qi and Northern Zhou. Just when it seemed that China would be forever divided into two cultural spheres, north and south, a new leader emerged.

## The Sui Empire

Yang Jiang was a distinguished official of the Northern Zhou and a member of the extended imperial family. Perhaps tired of the excesses of Emperor Xuan, his son-in-law, and realizing his own superior capabilities, Yang Jiang took advantage of Xuan's early death to seize control of the state, becoming Emperor Wen of Sui.

As Emperor Wen, he immediately exercised his powers to initiate a period of transformation. Legalism was given a place of honor in his court above Confucianism, and his personal religion of Buddhism was heavily patronized. A new system of bureaucracy was instituted, which served as the template of all future Chinese imperial administrations. Wen confiscated large private landholdings and leased them back to the peasantry, collecting taxes on their produce. Alongside this redistribution of land, he initiated the construction of massive granaries to stabilize the price and availability of grain. With the agricultural base of his Empire reestablished, he improved his military in readiness for his ultimate objective: the conquest of the Chen Dynasty of the south.

With the state treasury almost empty, Wen succeeded in wielding a force of overwhelming power against the Chen state. In a strategy reminiscent of the Jin defeat of Wu, more than 500,000 soldiers, supported by thousands of warships, were assembled by the Sui Empire along the northern banks of the Yangtze. Faced with a coordinated assault across such a long front, the Chen Empire soon capitulated, and, for the first time in almost three hundred years, China was reunified (Keay, 2009).

# CHAPTER 4
## *ENTER A GOLDEN AGE*

A famous tale from the Tang Dynasty illustrates the unique character of the period:

*The Emperor turned to the monk, her face quizzical. "Can you provide an example?" she said.*

*"Of course," replied Fazang, the monk. He stood plainly before her, his head humbly shaved, his robes pale orange. "I have already prepared a*

*room, please come."*

*Her curiosity piqued, she stood and followed, dismissing the protests of her courtiers with a wave of her hand.*

*"See this candle?" Fazang said. "This represents the relationship of the One to the Many."*

*Walking ahead of her, he placed the candle on a plinth at the center of the darkened room.*

*Her breath caught in her throat when she realized that the room was full of mirrors, each one reflecting the warm light of the candle.*

*Smiling, Fazang then placed a polished crystal in front of the candle. It sparkled with a thousand radiant points of light. "And this represents the relationship of the Many to the One."*


The above passage shows the female Chinese Emperor questioning a Sogdian monk on the esoteric metaphysics of Indian religion (Talbot, 1991). It is fair to say that such an occurrence was unprecedented in Chinese history.


## Founding of the Tang

Emperor Wen of Sui had left the newly reunified Empire in a position of strength, but his son, Emperor Yangdi, was not to reign as wisely. As did his father, Yangdi continued not only to patronize Buddhism and the Arts but also to invest in massive construction projects. The Grand Canal, initiated by his father, was completed, connecting eastern China from Hangzhou in the south to Zhangzhou in the north. To celebrate its completion, Yangdi toured the canal triumphantly at the head of a flotilla of barges tens of miles long.

The Grand Canal had been completed by female forced laborers—the pool of male workers devastated by horrendous casualty rates—and this combination of exploitation of labor and personal extravagance typified his reign. Resentments began to build in the populace, and three massive failed invasions of the state of Goguryeo in what is now Korea led to open rebellion. Yangdi fled to the south of China, where he was assassinated. One of his generals, Li Yuan, took advantage of the power vacuum to declare himself Emperor Gaozu of the Tang dynasty (Wright, 2011).

## Early Achievements

Emperor Gaozu busied himself with undoing the harm done to the populace by Emperor Yangdi of Sui. As re-established by Emperor Wen of Sui, the equal fields system of government land distribution was extended across the Empire, ensuring that all available land was cultivated, that the peasantry was financially solvent, and that large private monopolies could not develop. Agricultural innovations including waterwheels and improved plows increased the ease of production, and life for the common people of the Empire became better than ever.

Gaozu's reign lasted for eight years before turbulent events forced his hand. His second son Li Shimin, a man of driving ambition who had helped his father carve out the victory as the Sui dynasty collapsed, had killed two of his brothers and all of their sons. Unable to control his son, and fearful of what he would do next, Gaozu abdicated the throne.

Li Shimin's bloody rise might seem like the prelude to a reign of terror, but as Emperor

Taizong of Tang, he proved himself to be an exceptionally capable ruler, perhaps more than any Emperor who had come before him. A student of history, he was driven by a personal mission to build a lasting Empire, unlike that of the Sui that he had helped to overthrow. One of his first acts on ascending the throne was to free 6000 serving girls of the court to allow them to live free lives and marry. He also did away with other costly and frivolous court expenses and spectacles. Taizong continued his father's series of reforms and employed people of merit, regardless of political or ethnic background, to serve as his ministers. In a step that would have had Qin Shi Huang Di, the First Emperor, rolling in his terracotta-lined grave, he allowed his ministers to openly criticize him (Bo, 1991).

It was not only court life that was more open and expressive during Taizong's time, but Chinese society as a whole also became more outward-looking. The Tang Emperors were descended from both "barbarian" nomads and ethnic Han and held both ethnic groups in equal esteem. The capital of the empire, Chang'an, was a metropolis filled with people from all across East Asia and even farther afield. The Japanese and Koreans sent delegations to the Tang capital and were so awed that they took many aspects of Tang society for their own. The southern Korean kingdom of Silla used the Imperial bureaucracy as a template. Kimonos, the tea ceremony, and wood-block printing, so typically Japanese to the modern eye, trace their origin to Tang China. The ancient Japanese capital of Nara was even purpose-built in imitation of Chang'an (Wright, 2011).

Taizong's ambition did not end at improving the lives of the common people, he wanted to put an end to the nomadic depredations that had blighted Chinese history. As a Turkic speaker with Turkic blood, he understood how to defeat the tribes of the steppes. By 630 CE, he had forced the Eastern Turks to acknowledge him as "Heavenly Khan" above their own leadership. He then deployed the Turks along the northern border as a guardian force of the Chinese Empire, using their mobility and aggression to perfect advantage.

Just before Taizong launched his assault on the nomads, one man took advantage of the calm before the storm to journey west. Xuanzang, a monk and brilliant scholar, had become frustrated with the existing translations of Buddhist literature. Xuanzang set off for India, on a horse, and with a drunk guide, on a mission to learn all that he could about the life and teachings of the Buddha. For seventeen years he toured and studied, and, when he finally returned to China, he was one of the most celebrated intellectuals in all of Asia, riding at the head of a baggage train gifted by kings and emperors. His work revolutionized the understanding of Buddhism in East Asia and his life and journey became a celebrated aspect of Chinese culture (Cao & Sun, 2011).

## The Reign of Empress Wu

Taizong's son Emperor Gaozung, unlike his father, was not an extroverted leader and fearless warrior; in fact, he was famed for his poor health and timid nature. The person of suitable ambition in the Imperial family at this time was, in fact, his favored consort, Wu. Wu rose steadily, first becoming a full Empress, with her children promoted to be first in line for the throne, then subsequently, making decisions for Emperor Gaozung as his health failed him. When he died, she installed two of her sons in succession as puppet Emperors.

Eventually, her grip on the throne secure, she tired of this charade of regency. In 690 CE, she proclaimed herself Emperor Wu of the Zhou dynasty, becoming China's first, and history's only, female Emperor. Wu continued her forebears' policies of supporting agriculture and silk production and took a hands-on role in the imperial administration, often serving as an examiner herself. In this way, she was able to fill her administration with rising talent drawn from low to middle-status families from across China—people who were more likely to be loyal to her than would the offspring of high-ranking families. China prospered, and the population rose from 3.8 million at the outset of her reign to 6.15 million by its close (Cao & Sun, 2011).

Wu's court was a colorful place, and she took a special interest in the teachings of mystics and sages from many various cultures. The arts were lavishly supported, and Wu herself composed books of poetry. She elevated Daoism's *Dao de Jing* to become the curriculum of the Imperial examinations. She also funded the carving of the Vairocana Buddha at the Longmen Grottoes; an exquisite monument regarded by posterity as the quintessence of Tang-era stonework. Viewing herself as a living savior, Wu's identification with Buddhism was so complete that a famous Buddhist monk called Huaiyi was, rather scandalously, rumored to be her lover (Keay, 2011).

While Emperor Wu was undoubtedly merciless in her subjugation or destruction of all who opposed her, however, we cannot be sure of the truth of her reign, as her histories were written by men, the majority of whom resented her inversion of the Confucian order of things. This is a fact that Wu herself would take in her stride. On hearing the words of the poem, *A Call to Crusade Against Wu Zetian* by Luo Binwang, one of the greatest poets of her day, she smiled, praised the poem's composition, and asked why the court had not hired him (Cao & Sun, 2011).

## Late Achievements

The Tang Empire was restored when, aged 81, Emperor Wu's health began to fail her and she was unable to prevent the restoration of the authority of her former puppet ruler son, Emperor Zhongzhong. Her other former puppet ruler son, Emperor Ruizong, followed in his place, but it was not until Ruizong's son Emperor Xuanzong inherited the throne in 713 CE that the Tang Dynasty would reach its zenith.

The infrastructure projects initiated by the Sui

and the following years of good governance of the Tang had led to China becoming the driving force behind Old World trade. Along the Silk Road and through the ports of the south, a variety of goods, people, and ideas flowed into China. In turn, Chinese porcelain and textiles were exported in a circulatory exchange. The Tang Empire was undoubtedly the most advanced and powerful civilization in the world, and its capital Chang'an the largest and most glorious city.

Xuanzong's reign was a celebrated time in Chinese history, however, through poor decision-making towards the end of his life, he sowed the seeds of the dynasty's eventual demise. He took an interest in one of his son's concubines, Yang Guifei, and gave many special privileges to her and her extended family. When an uprising of Khitan nomads in the northeast threatened the Empire, Xuanzong entrusted too much power to one of Yang Guifei's allies, An

Lushan, a general who had excelled in combating the steppe menace (Wright, 2011).

# CHAPTER 5
## *A DYNASTY BESET BY ENEMIES*

---

The 13th century was a time of great change on the steppes, precipitated by the actions of one man:

*High on the mountain, he makes his sacrifice; pouring the steaming mare's milk onto the stone like the first rays of the rising sun strike the earth. With his belt and hat drawn humbly round his neck, he offers his total submission, beating his chest and then prostrating himself before the risen sun.*

*The man's name is Temujin, and on this sacred peak, he has sworn to spend his life embodying the will of Tengri, the Great Sky God.*

*His destiny is not only to unify the tribes of the Mongols; it is to conquer all under the Sky.*

We know such intimate details of Temujin's life because they were recorded in a document known as *The Secret History of the Mongols* (Man, 2014). This warlord would change the destiny not only of the steppe tribes but also that of all Eurasia.

## Establishment

A Lushan, Xuanzhong's formerly-trusted

general, rebelled against the Tang overlordship in the year 755 CE, initiating a period of chaos across China. To combat his rebellion, increased power was devoted to regional military governors, who later were reluctant to relinquish their powers and privileges. In the following century, the inability of the Imperial administration and the corrupt military governors to cope with famine on the Yellow River resulted in a peasant rebellion breaking out under the charismatic leadership of a smuggler named Huang Chao. Huang Chao's bandits plundered their way across China, capturing the southern city of Guangzhou, massacring its foreign merchants. The Tang government was forced to employ steppe nomads to quell Huang Chao's rebellion, and by 907 CE, it had lost all authority. Across China, the governors seized regional power as neighboring tribal unions swept in to contest the spoils. As it had done before in the wake of the collapse of the Western Jin dynasty, China broke apart.

The years 907 CE to 960 CE are known to history as the era of the *Five Dynasties and 10 Kingdoms*. Five states claiming imperial overlordship rose and fell in the north, whereas the south split into dozens of smaller kingdoms. Eventually, this period of incessant conflict was brought to a close when a general from the Zhou Dynasty of the north declared himself Emperor Taizu of the Song. Within nineteen years, Taizu had conquered the kingdoms of the south and China was almost whole again (Keay, 2009).

## Hostile Neighbors

The world in which Taizu came to power was not the same world that had been dominated by the Tang. The Khitan, one of the many groups of steppe nomads that fringed the Chinese world, had carved out a state in the northeast, dominating a region that included present-day Beijing, Manchuria, and Mongolia. They declared this state the Liao Empire.

The Liao Empire was not a simple tribal confederacy like its ancient Xiongnu predecessors. Rather, it was a state partly modeled on Chinese culture in control of a largely settled populace, including many ethnic Han. The Liao had nothing to fear from Song China, and in 1004 CE, the Liao Empire launched an invasion.

Emperor Zhenzong, a successor to Emperor Taizong, was able to repel the invasion, but at the cost of a peace treaty that saw Song China paying the Liao Empire 100,000 taels (with one tael equivalent to 50 grams) of silver and 200,000 pieces of silk each year. Shortly after this capitulation, a Tibetan people known as the Tangut seized the area around the northern loop of the Yellow River and declared themselves the Xi Xia Empire.

The former Empire of the Tang was now split between three powerful states. Peace treaties maintained a balance of power, and society in each of the states progressed. Despite the contractual tribute leaving the treasury of Song China each year, the Liao Empire used its wealth to buy products from the Song, stimulating the economies of both Empires. The amount of land under cultivation in the Liao Empire greatly increased, as did its population. The state of Xi Xia expanded irrigation across the desert of the northwest and became a leading center of manufacturing—the technology of its furnaces and the quality of its metalwork were considered without equal. In Song China, the privatization of land enabled a system of land tenancy and contract labor to grow up. With more people than ever free to find employment that suited their particular talents, economic activity boomed across all sectors, and the population peaked at one hundred million

(Kerr, 2013).

This era of relative tranquility lasted for a century until events in the steppe tipped the fragile balance.

## Northern and Southern Song

The Khitan Liao ruled over many other ethnic groups, including the semi-nomadic Jurchen of what is now known as Manchuria. Resenting the government of their Khitan overlords, the Jurchens rebelled, and by 1120 CE, they had captured the Liao capital and declared their own rulership: the Jin Dynasty.

Sensing the opportunity to land a devastating blow on their Liao rivals, the Song allied themselves with the Jurchen. In a coordinated assault from the north and south, the forces of the Khitan Liao were broken between the hammer of the Jurchen army and the anvil of the Song army. It seemed like a great victory for the Song Empire, but their poor performance during the war—the Khitan Liao had not been broken on the anvil but had instead broken through Song lines and escaped west—had revealed to the Jurchen the weaknesses of the Song administration and its military (Chen, 2018).

In 1125 CE, the Jin Empire swept into Song territory, seized the capital, and captured Qinzong, the Song Emperor. Those members of the Song court who survived the invasion fled south of the Yangtze River, and Zhao Gou, a half-brother to the captured Emperor Qinzong, was installed as Emperor Gaozong. The Southern Song, as they would now be known, were able to hold their territory in the south of China and along the Yangtze River basin against the continued menace of Jin, but the historic heartland of China—the middle and lower

Yellow River and the North China Plain—was now lost. For the first time in recorded history, China was ruled over by non-Han ethnic people.

It was perhaps because of this blow that Chinese society in Southern Song times became more insular and introspective. Gone was the love of exotica typified by the Tang, and Chinese society began to reject foreign influences. Buddhism, a foreign religion, lost its place of honor at court, and Confucianism underwent a resurgence. Guided by a series of brilliant thinkers, Neo-Confucianism provided an indigenous Chinese response to the cosmological and metaphysical questions originally posed by Buddhism (Zhang, 2015). Daoism also became more organized, and scripture based as it competed with Buddhist temples for patronage and esteem.

Despite the loss of the north, historically the most advanced and populous area of China, and the ongoing antagonistic relationship with Jin, a society under the Southern Song continued to progress in astonishing ways. Advances in shipbuilding and navigation meant that ocean-worthy Chinese vessels traded across the South China Sea and the Indian Ocean. Inland waterways were patrolled by boats driven by paddled wheels. To support the volume of long-distance trade, the concept of insurance was invented, as was the act of printing paper currency. Gunpowder had been refined from a curiosity into an effective weapon of war, and the Song army was equipped with fire arrows, fire lances (the progenitor of the handgun), grenades, cannons, and flamethrowers (Kerr, 2013).

New varieties of rice imported from Southeast Asia allowed double or triple harvests, and agricultural output increased to the degree that the market could support millions of people involved in a variety of fields, such as tailors, teachers, craftsmen, physicians, merchants, and entertainers. The average citizen of China was able to enjoy more leisure time, and, perhaps more importantly, had more spending power than ever before; as a consequence, urban life was vibrant, and tea houses, operas, bookshops, markets, and hotels thrived across the land (Cao & Sun, 2011).

At a time when Europe was just emerging from the Early Middle Ages, Southern Song society was undoubtedly the most advanced and prosperous in the world.

# The Mongol Terror

The steppes of Eurasia stretch in a band across the Old World, from Manchuria in the east, to Ukraine in the west. Bounded by forests to the north, and deserts and mountain ranges to the south, this area of rolling grassland had for millennia been a highly fluid region where tribes of nomadic horsemen competed for control. The fluidity of these tribal confederacies was a result of the wide-open expanse of the land and the horse lords' nomadic nature. Little did the people of the Southern Song know that, in these northern steppes, a storm was rising. The eye of that storm was a man: born as Temujin yet known to history as Genghis Khan.

At the time of Genghis Khan's birth in 1206 CE, the Mongols were a minor tribe of the far north steppe, under the nominal control of the Jin Dynasty. Temujin, a charismatic leader, and outstanding strategist unified the various tribes of the surrounding steppes and transformed their organization from a collection of tribes into an army united under his command.

It was an army that he immediately put to use, employing its unparalleled maneuverability and potential to wage war across multiple fronts to conduct raids, plundering the vulnerable areas of his more sedentary neighbors. Genghis' warriors would emerge unheralded from the wastelands and deserts, striking a target and then retreating. The Mongol army was entirely mounted, and so it was far too swift to be engaged by any opposition forces that fielded infantry. They were armed with a composite bow that could launch arrows up to 500m, out-ranging, and out-performing Chinese crossbows and fire lances. The Mongols were a superior fighting force, even compared to the elite cavalry of the Xi Xia and Jin (Man, 2014).

Mongol raiders terrorized the Empires of the Tangut and the Jurchen, gaining territory and exacting tribute, but the first nation to fall was Kara Khitai, the Central Asian successor state founded by remnants of the Liao Dynasty. The ruler of Khwarezmia, a powerful Islamic nation on the coast of the Caspian Sea, then made the mistake of killing a Mongol envoy, and Genghis Khan's attention thus turned westward. So began a fourteen-year military campaign that left the former glory of Khwarezmian civilization in ashes and the Mongols as the uncontested masters of Central Asia.

According to some sources, in 1227 CE, Genghis fell from his horse and succumbed to his injuries (Man, 2014). His death did not mark the end of the Mongol Khanate. Instead, it marked a renewal of the Mongolian will to conquer the world. Ultimately, this desire for conquest and vengeance was carried out by his son and successor, Ogedei.

# CHAPTER 6
## *THE MONGOLS RULE CHINA*

---

In the 13th century, China, or Cathay as it was known to the people of medieval Europe, was a place of utter mystery for Europeans. With direct routes to China blocked either by steppe nomads or the rival civilization of Islam, all Europe knew of China was the exquisite nature of the products that made it along the Silk Road to the markets of Constantinople, Venice, and Rome. Of the realities of life in China itself, they only heard rumors upon rumors. For example, many Europeans erroneously yet legitimately believed that traveling to China would mean crossing a land ruled by people with the heads of dogs (Beazley, 1903).

The veil of mystery separating East from West was torn asunder in a most terrible way, when in 1241 CE, Mongol forces, in the space of only two days, destroyed the armies of both Poland and Hungary. The kingdoms and principalities of Europe were shaken to their core, and the Pope deployed an envoy to meet with the Great Khan, who now ruled an Empire that bordered his own spiritual domain. Giovanni del Carpine, an overweight, middle-aged friar, was given this epic task, and after three months of exhausting travel, he succeeded in reaching the court of the Great Khan at the Karakorum, high on the Mongolian Plateau. Ogodei had died, and del Carpine was able to witness the inauguration of his son, Guyuk, as the new Great Khan. Del

Carpine presented Guyuk with a letter from the Pope and extended an invitation to baptize him as a Christian. Guyuk declined, responding that the Pope and all the kings of Europe must come and pay tribute to him, Guyuk, Khan of Khans (Beazley, 1903).

## Marco Polo

The Mongol conquest of Asia had created the *Pax Mongolica*; an era of relative peace in the lands ruled by the Great Khan. It was now much simpler for a European to reach the fabled East. One enterprising Venetian family, the Polos, set off in 1271 CE to explore the Silk Road, and, unlike Giovanni del Carpine, reached China proper; after four years of travel, they arrived at Dadu, city of the Great Khan, known in the modern-day as Beijing.

The Polos had not been idle during their long and often interrupted journey across Asia, and by the time they were given an audience with the Great Khan were able to converse with him in Mongolian, his native tongue. This fact, along with young Marco's youth and intelligence, gained the Great Khan's favor, and Marco was employed as an agent and emissary of his government (Bergreen, 2007).

This story may sound like a completely fantastical turn of events—that a lowly merchant from the opposite end of the earth could find a place of high employment under the most powerful ruler in the world—but the policy of the Mongol government was to employ someone ethnically non-Han to oversee the Han. The Mongol population, numbering in the hundreds of thousands, ruled over a Han population numbering in the tens of millions—so, fearing rebellion, they appointed ethnic minorities drawn from across their vast Empire as administrators to aid in their control of the Han majority (Keay, 2009).

## Kublai's China

The Great Khan at the time of Marco's arrival in China was Kublai, grandson of Genghis, and the first person of non-Han ethnicity to rule the entirety of China. As Great Khan, Kublai's personal domain stretched from the Pacific Ocean in the east, to Lake Baikal in the north, to Vietnam in the south, to the Pamir mountains in the west. His Khanate was the senior partner in a Mongol confederacy—The Chagatai Khanate, Ilkhanate, and Khanate of the Golden Horde—together made up the largest land Empire in history (Wright, 2011). To an awed young Marco, meeting Kublai was like encountering a living Caesar or Alexander the Great, and this comparison was entirely accurate.

Kublai reigned in splendor from Dadu, his newly constructed capital. It was a city that astonished Marco; a multi-ethnic and multireligious metropolis filled with the best and brightest from across the huge empire. Unlike European cities of the time, it had not grown up organically—cobbled together in response to the vagaries of war and fortune—nor was it filled with squalor. It had been planned and purpose-built; laid out on a grid with huge, straight, tree-lined avenues. Water flowed systematically through the city's rivers, lakes, and canals, flushing away refuse, cooling the air, and irrigating the land around (Man, 2014).

Within the city were parks filled with rare white animals of all kinds, including stags, squirrels, and ermine. White, symbolizing heaven, was the color of Kublai's Yuan Dynasty. Even more spectacular was the palace itself, a fortress within the fortress of a city. Its interior walls were emblazoned with artworks made from silver and gold, and its halls were grand enough to seat thousands of revelers. Even the roofing was spectacular; crystalline tiles shone under the sun, reflecting all the colors of the rainbow.

As an agent of the Great Khan, Marco was able to access this inner world of delights, bearing witness to feasts and festivals on a scale that defied his provincial imagination. Here, Marco engaged in political and theological debates, observed how the country was governed and was left dumbfounded by the sexual stamina of Kublai's attendance to several wives and several *hundred* concubines (Bergreen, 2007).

Marco served under Kublai Khan for 17 years, during which he was sent across China, and to several neighboring countries of Asia, serving as a tax collector and ambassador. On his eventual return to Venice, he dictated the stories of his travels, providing Europe with many details of life in "Cathay". A keen observer, he would provide much information unbelieved by his contemporaries, but corroborated in the light of later knowledge:

> "All the people and regions of men who are under his rule gladly take these sheets in payment, because wherever they go they make all their payments with them both for goods and for pearls and for precious stones and for gold and for silver; they can buy everything with them, and they make payment with the sheets of which I have told you."
>
> - Marco Polo (Bergreen, 2007)

For Marco, more impressive than even the extraordinary wealth of the Mongol court was this strange "alchemy" where gold was converted to paper and then back again. It would be another four hundred years before

Europe was ready to embrace this particular innovation. Paper currency had been a feature of life in Song dynasty China, but one of Kublai's innovations on ascending the throne was to expand the system throughout his Empire (Man, 2014).

## Victory and Consolidation

In 1260 CE, when Kublai became Khan of Khans following a succession conflict with his brother, the Southern Song Dynasty was still intact. Song China, populous, fortified, and possessing a gunpowder-armed army and navy, was a resolute foe. Conquest of the Korean peninsula and the Dali kingdom in what is now the Yunnan province in southwest China enabled Kublai's forces to surround and outflank the Song. After sixteen years of fighting, employing infantry armies composed of Han conscripts, supported by siege engine technology learned from the Ilkhanate's wars in the Middle East, Kublai

Khan triumphed.


The Song Dowager Empress surrendered, and Kublai, in a break from Mongol tradition, treated the deposed royal court of the Song well and forbade his armies to massacre the civilians of the Song capital of Lin'an (modern Hangzhou). More intellectually inclined than many of his Mongol contemporaries, and educated from a young age by Chinese luminaries, Kublai saw himself as not only the Khan of Khans but also as the rightful Emperor of China. Taizong, the great Emperor of the Tang, who ruled as both Emperor of the Chinese and Heavenly Khan of the steppe, was his model for governance, and Kublai set himself the task of building an effective Empire (Bergreen, 2007).


The Mongol postal service—a series of stations served by relay riders—that kept all corners of the great steppe Empire in constant communication with one another was extended across China. Waterways, including the linking of the Grand Canal to Dadu, were improved and extended, as were roads. All currency in circulation was seized and a new Mongol paper currency was issued. In time, three forms of Mongol paper currency were in use in Yuan China, and these currencies were protected against inflation or depreciation by being exchangeable on a 1:1 basis with a set amount of silver or silk. Schools and hospitals were built and a new Imperial Observatory, utilizing the knowledge of the Islamic world, was founded (Man, 2014).

Yuan China was now the driving force and center of a trading network that reached to the ends of Eurasia.

## Quest for Expansion

Before becoming Great Khan, Kublai had distinguished himself as a military strategist during his early years, campaigning against the Southern Song. As Emperor of the Yuan Dynasty, his quest to fulfill his grandfather's vision of Mongol domination of the world did not lessen, and his rule was marked by a series of military campaigns aimed at subjugating all neighboring territories.

Although he was able to comprehensively defeat the Southern Song, the subsequent campaigns launched by Kublai were less successful. Vietnam was invaded three times but managed to repel the Mongols on every occasion. In 1274 CE, an invasion of Japan failed, and in response, Kublai ordered the construction of an even larger invasion force comprising 1,400 boats manned by 140,000 soldiers. In 1281 CE, this fleet attacked the island of Kyushu and the

Mongols once again encountered stiff and effective resistance from the Japanese. The two sides were locked in a stalemate when the divine wind or *Kamikaze* arrived—a great typhoon that smashed the Mongol ships to matchwood against the Japanese shore (Bergreen, 2007).

Not only had the Mongol Yuan lost the majority of its naval power, but the aura of Mongol invincibility of the preceding decades had also been shattered. Kublai would only have the will to conduct one more overseas raid; a punitive mission to Java in 1293 CE that also ended in failure.

In 1294 CE, following Kublai's death, the Mongol Yuan became less willing to project their military force. Although diminished, the Khanate was still the world's wealthiest and most powerful civilization. If his successors had taken as much care over internal statecraft as

Kublai did, then perhaps the Yuan Dynasty may have endured. As it happened, the Mongol leaders increasingly ruled like parasites on top of a nest; content to live extravagantly on the wealth produced by the Chinese people while becoming less and less invested in the lives and well-being of the regular citizens (Kerr, 2013).

Under the Mongol Yuan, the Han Chinese were essentially second-class citizens. They could not own weapons, and even access to sharp kitchen implements was limited. The secret police were appointed to every village, watching and listening for signs of revolt, and strict curfews on night-time movements and public gatherings were enforced. Probably most insulting of all for the proud Han people, they were denied access to the machinery of government, as the Mongols preferred to employ non-Han people to administer their Empire whenever possible (Keay, 2009).

Tensions in the populace rose throughout the reign of every subsequent Yuan Emperor, and by 1351 CE, less than a century after Kublai's death, they had reached a breaking point.

# CHAPTER 7
# *THE MIGHTY MING*

---

Life for the common people during the final years of the Yuan was hard:

*Zhu Yuanzhang, aged 16, and his brother buried their father first. They dug the grave themselves, wrapped his emaciated body in white linen, and laid him to rest. Next, they buried their mother, then their younger sister, then their older brother. All laid far below so that the wild dogs would not find them. Each was wrapped in white cloth.*

*Zhu Yuanzhang and his brother were now alone in the world, but they were not alone—everyone in the valley had spent the winter burying loved ones. Those that could find the strength dug into the cold, hard earth. Some families had gone completely, with no one left to dig the graves.*

*What now? What to do? Where to go? Perhaps only the Buddha could understand the reason for such suffering.*

From the humblest of origins, Zhu Yuanzhang would go on to distinguish himself during this age of great upheaval (Kerr, 2013).

## Red Turbans and White Lotus

The early 14th century was a time of crisis in the lands of the Yuan Dynasty. The country was wracked by plague, flood, and famine. One epidemic, lasting from 1331 to 1333 CE, resulted in the deaths of 13 million people. There were further mass outbreaks of disease in the 1340s, 1350s, and 1360s (Sussman, 2011). For the people of the time, it must have seemed like the world was ending, and, as a result, many turned to religion for answers. One sect, the White Lotus, that preached that a Buddhist savior figure was soon to arrive on earth, became especially popular.

In the 1330s, a Buddhist monk and follower of the White Lotus named Peng Yingyu organized an uprising. He was soon caught and executed by the Yuan. Peng Yingyu died, but his adoption of Red Turbans to identify militant members of the sect persisted, and from 1351 CE Red Turban rebellions became common throughout China (Twitchett, 1998).

It was during one such rebellion in 1352 CE that Yuan soldiers burned the monastery of another monk—the now 24-year-old Zhu Yuanzhang. Consequently, he joined the Red Turbans, where his confidence, communication abilities, and intelligence-led to a rapid promotion through the ranks. In 1356 CE, at the head of a peasant army, he captured Nanjing, one of the major cities of southern China.

By 1363 CE, his forces were strong enough to achieve victory in the battle of lake Poyang—perhaps the largest naval battle in recorded history—and his control of the Yangtze River valley was assured. Year by year, Zhu Yuanzhang's forces won victory after victory, extending their territory across China. In 1367 CE, he issued a proclamation stating that the

Mongol Yuan had lost the Mandate of Heaven. The statement was a powerful propagandistic victory for Zhu Yuanzhang and his followers; after all, who could doubt the inauspicious ruination of recent years? Zhu Yuanzhang's epic victories and nascent state-managed on Neo-Confucian principles stood in stark contrast to the weakening, corrupt, and foreign regime of the Mongol Yuan. In 1368 CE, when his armies entered Dadu, they were unopposed, the Yuan court having fled.

Zhu Yuanzhang declared himself Hongwu, Emperor of the Ming (meaning "Bright") Dynasty and set about the task of revitalizing the country. Hongwu understood better than anyone a lot of the peasant class, and he immediately took steps to lessen their burden. The duty of tax collection and law enforcement was assigned to the wealthiest and most senior villagers, lessening corruption. The tax system was overhauled, and tax breaks were given to those who brought uncultivated land into cultivation. Stipulations for a proportion of land to be dedicated to cash crops ensured a supply of materials and finance for the cottage industry. The importance of the Confucian values guiding this reorganization was emphasized, and imperial decrees promoting good and filial conduct were posted in every village and every town across the country.


Confucianism regained its place of dominance at court, and the imperial examination system and method of governance were re-instituted. Wary of the threat of the Yuan court, which still existed in its heartland of Mongolia, Hongwu built a strong military but innovated the process of army selection and assembly so that neither his generals nor their soldiers were stationed together long-term, thus lessening the ability of the generals to become regional warlords.

Taken solely on the merits of his reign, Hongwu would seem a legendary, almost divine, hero of Chinese culture. But he had a dark side; from the beginning of his rise to power, it became clear that he would kill anyone who opposed him. This fear and paranoia manifested during his reign in the form of much-feared secret police, and a punitive regime with more in common with the excesses of the Legalist first Emperor Qin Shi Huang Di than the Confucian virtues and Buddhist beneficence that Hongwu preached (Kerr, 2013).

# China Ascendant

The course of Hongwu's succession did not run smooth, and Hongwu's fourth son seized the throne, becoming Emperor Yongle of the Ming. Like his father before him, Emperor Yongle was a ruthless yet visionary man. He transferred the capital north to Beiping (now known as Beijing), where he began construction of the Forbidden City, a massive imperial palace complex that still stands to this day. The Grand Canal, which had fallen into disrepair in the later years of the

Yuan, was renovated, and an extension of the canal was built to supply grain to the capital. With the agricultural base of the country secure, Yongle asserted Ming China's military power, spending many years of his reign at war with Mongol Yuan to the north, and, in a unique period of Chinese dynastic history, projecting the force of China's navy out across the seas (Wright, 2011).

## An Age of Exploration

Zheng He was a Muslim man born in Yunnan province, at that time under Mongol Yuan control. During the wars of Ming expansion, he was captured, castrated, and taken to serve by the Ming, being sent to the household of the Prince of Yan. During his time of service, he formed a strong bond with the Prince of Yan, and when the Prince of Yan overthrew his brother and became Yongle Emperor, Zheng He was elevated to the position of Grand Director of the palace.

In 1405 CE, the Emperor commanded that an expedition be set out to explore the western ocean. Zheng He was named Chief Envoy of this maritime mission, commanding 27,000 men and a fleet of 62 treasure ships. On Zheng He's first voyage, he sailed across the Indian Ocean to Sri Lanka and the southern tip of India. Pirate fleets were cleared from the seas, trading posts were established, and an Indian king who had the temerity to resist his diplomacy was captured.

Six such voyages were sponsored by the Yongle Emperor, diplomatically connecting the Ming Dynasty with kingdoms and principalities across South East Asia and the Indian Ocean, even as far afield as the eastern coast of Africa. Through these expeditions, Ming military primacy was projected across the known world's oceanic trading networks, extending the Imperial tributary system beyond states immediately neighboring China, and initiating a Ming government-controlled monopoly on international trade was established (Keay, 2009).

## Decline Into Crisis

Following the reign of the Yongle Emperor, Chinese civilization took another inward turn. Only one more Treasure Fleet was launched, and thereafter the Ming returned to the non-interventionist foreign policy of their founder, Hongwu. The Mongol Yuan remained a threat, and the Ming increasingly responded with defensive, rather than offensive, strategies—the Great Wall protecting the settled population from the steppe menace took its current form during Ming times (Cao & Sun, 2011).

For over 250 years, the Ming endured, but

during that time the achievements of Chinese culture were beginning to be eclipsed by the Europeans as they pursued their Age of Exploration. When one Jesuit missionary at the Imperial court showed the assembly a mechanical clock his Chinese observers were dumbfounded, not realizing that they, the Chinese, had invented the mechanical clock 900 years previously (Kerr, 2013).

Students of China's history will recognize a repeating pattern at the fall of an Imperial dynasty; corrupt officials, an ineffective central government, social catastrophe, and peasant uprisings. All of these factors became apparent in the early 17th century, the final years of Ming reign, perhaps exacerbated by the climate phenomenon known as "The Little Ice Age". During this time, China was subjected to summer droughts, winter freezes, and flooding. Famine broke out, and the Ming government, its treasury empty due to a combination of palace largesse and loss of control of international trade to the European powers, was unable to adequately respond.

In the face of famine, army deserters took to forming large gangs, marauding across the countryside in search of sustenance. The leader of one such group was a peasant named Li Zicheng, who in 1644 CE, marched into Beijing at the head of an army of tens of thousands of disgruntled commoners and ex-militia. Rather than face capture by the rebels, the last Emperor of the Ming Dynasty committed suicide, and Li Zicheng declared himself Emperor of the Shun Dynasty (Cao & Sun, 2011).

It was to be a short reign.

# CHAPTER 8
## *THE MAGNIFICENT QING*

•———————• • ● • • ———————•

The year 1644 CE saw a Ming general faced with one of the greatest dilemmas in recorded history:

*General Wu Sangui stood before the gate. Vast and black it was, spanning the width of the defile between the mountains. From where he stood, it was so large that it blocked out the light of the sun. Wu Sangui perspired. His sworn task was to guard the Ming Empire and its people from the terror that dwelt beyond the gate. The barbarous and merciless enemy on the other side of the Great Wall.*

*Today, an army stood beyond the gate, just outside. A force of tens of thousands of warriors, flying banners colored yellow, red, white, and blue. General Wu was about to do what he swore he never would. He felt the sweat drip from his chin. With a nod to his men, it was done. They began to turn the winches, and the hinges of the great gate creaked.*

*A chink of light appeared, widening to a flood.*

*The gate was open. He had let them through.*

Joining the usurping Shun Dynasty or allying with the steppe nomads he was duty-bound to repel, the consequences of General Wu Sangui's choice would echo down through the ages (Kerr, 2013).

## The Rise of the Manchus

The freezing cold of the "Little Ice Age" created much hardship for the Jurchen people who lived on the Manchurian plain to the northeast of Ming China. When the Ming state, blind to their suffering, demanded tribute of the usual amount, the Jurchen tribes began to rebel against Ming overlordship. After a period of internecine warfare on the Manchurian plain, one leader had achieved prominence: Nurhaci.

Nurhaci re-organized Jurchen society into four units, each with its own banner and color. These units functioned as both social and military organizations; in an echo of Genghis' exploits, Jurchen society had been fully mobilized for warfare. The Korean Joseon, the Mongols, and the Ming, all felt Nurhaci's wrath and, by 1616 CE, he had carved out a vast amount of territory in the northeast. Nurhaci was now powerful enough to declare himself Khan of the Jin Dynasty (often termed Later Jin to differentiate it from the earlier Jin Dynasty founded by his Jurchen ancestors).

In 1626 CE, Nurhaci died from injuries received in battle with the Ming, but he bequeathed to his sons a strong and well-organized state. His eighth son, Hong Taiji, extended the four banners system into eight, changed the name of the Jin Dynasty to the Qing Dynasty, and renamed the Jurchen people as the Manchu people. When Ming General Wu Sangui opened the gates of the Shanhai pass, Hong Taiji's younger brother, Prince Dorgon, swept through at the head of the most irresistible cavalry force in Asia.

Wu Sangui hoped that he had recruited a powerful ally for the Ming against Li Zicheng's peasant uprising, but the Manchu Qing had other ideas. Hong Taiji's five-year-old ninth son was installed as Shenzhen, first Emperor of the Qing Dynasty, and, reigning as regent, Prince Dorgon oversaw a two-decade-long series of military campaigns that ended in the conquest of the entirety of China (Kerr, 2013).

## The Beneficent Reign of Kangxi

Shenzhen's son Kangxi inherited a China restored but not pacified. Many Han Chinese resented the foreign regime of the Qing, and, in

1673 CE, the *Revolt of the Three Feudatories* broke out, led by three Han aristocrats from southern China. Kangxi's forces labored for eight years to crush the rebels, and in the aftermath, he took steps to consolidate Qing control of China and legitimize Qing reign in the eyes of his Han subjects.

By lowering land taxes and prohibiting the practice of land seizure by aristocratic creditors, Kangxi aided the common people. These changes had increased the amount of land under cultivation and stimulated the economy. Indeed, by the late period of his reign, Kangxi was able to free the peasantry completely from land taxation and froze the practice of forced labor.

He promoted, and perhaps more importantly, practiced Confucianism, holding it in a place of esteem at his court. He also commissioned vast works of literature, including a new Chinese dictionary, a grand history of the Ming Dynasty, and the largest book of Chinese poetry ever compiled. As well as patronizing indigenous Chinese culture, Kangxi was open-minded enough to learn from the European diplomats at his court, even becoming the first Chinese Emperor to learn how to play the harpsichord (Kerr, 2013).

This cultural transmission was a two-way street, and details of Chinese civilization learned from returning missionaries and diplomats caused as much of a sensation in Europe as did the brilliant quality of Qing porcelain and textiles. The greatest intellectuals of the European Age of Enlightenment, men such as Voltaire, Hume, and Leibniz, held the philosophies and culture of China in high esteem (Wright, 2011).

Kangxi was a driven man, whose habit of waking

early and sleeping late, attending almost constantly to affairs of state, was more similar to that of a 20th century President than that of the pampered autocrats of earlier dynasties. The restored Ming system of imperial administration continued under Kangxi, but he also installed a parallel system whereby regional governors could communicate directly with him; thus, news that would have been filtered out by the imperial administration system under past regimes made its way directly to him, without their knowledge or interference (Spence, 2013).

In addition to being cultured and learned, Kangxi was not afraid to lead; he took personal control of the military campaign against the Dzungars, another group of steppe nomads who had been raiding his northwestern borders and emerged victoriously. During his reign, Taiwan and Mongolia would be incorporated into the Qing Empire, and the growing threat of the

Russians, then in the midst of their conquest of Siberia, would be checked by the actions of Qing troops at the Amur River, preventing loss of the Pacific seaboard to the Tsars (Finer, 1999).

When Kangxi died in 1722 CE, Qing China was a huge, populous, multi-ethnic, and rich empire. It was the envy of the European powers whose diplomats flocked to the imperial court—competing for its favor and its trade. It was the envy of the world.

## The Glorious Reign of Qianlong

Kangxi's son, Emperor Yongzheng, proved himself as diligent and capable as his father, and his reign was notable for its burgeoning peace and prosperity. His foresight stretched to matters of posterity. When he passed away suddenly in 1735 CE, he had already written the name of his chosen successor within a sealed and locked wooden box. When the box was opened in front of the imperial family, and its contents revealed, rulership was passed to his fourth son, who was enthroned as the Qianlong Emperor.

It soon became apparent that Yongzheng had chosen well, as Qianlong, like his father and grandfather before him, proved a devoted, energetic, and intelligent leader of the vast Empire. He undertook extensive tours of his Empire; on each trip, he was accompanied with beautiful scroll paintings on which he would write notes and poetry. If Europeans had the ideal of the Renaissance man, then Qianlong was the eastern equivalent; beloved by Confucians for his genteel nature and erudition, famed amongst the Manchus for his martial prowess (Kerr, 2013).

Qianlong continued his father and grandfather's campaigns against the Dzungars, eventually extending his domination of the steppe as far as Lake Balkhash in present-day Kazakhstan. Tibet was also incorporated, extending the Empire's domination over more than 4.5 million square miles of territory (Taagepera, 1997). This was more expansive than ever before—and the neighboring states of Nepal, Burma, Siam, Laos, Vietnam, and the Philippines demonstrated their submission by sending yearly tributes to the Qing court.

Qianlong abdicated the throne in order not to reign longer than his beloved grandfather, Kangxi, however, he remained the power behind the throne until his death in 1796 CE. It was during his later years that he would flatly refuse British appeals for a trade deal, and, despite his friendly relationships with western missionaries at court, would remain opposed to Christian expansion within China, as well as being generally suspicious of any outside forces that wished to influence his Empire. Qianlong's attitude to the European trading powers that now encircled his borders would characterize that of his Qing successors (Kerr, 2013).

To the Chinese, the reign of Qianlong was long (the longest, if including his time as retired Emperor) and glorious, but as with all histories, this is the view from a certain perspective. For the Muslim community of China, his reign was noted for lessened opportunities and increased discrimination (Elverskog, 2010), and for the Dzungars, his campaigns were tantamount to genocide (Perdue, 2005).

## Encroaching Enemies

General George Macartney, head of the trading mission that was refused by Qianlong, took voluminous notes on life in Qianlong's China, including on the weaknesses of the Qing military as compared to the British. It was knowledge that the European trading powers, locked in competition for a commercial opportunity, at first did not act upon.

While Qing China was content to sit at the center of a network of foreign tributary states, Europe had been undergoing a transformation from an Age of Discovery to an Age of Empire. The major powers now controlled vast colonial territories and their insatiable industrial economies depended on a constant expansion of colonial extraction. Science and industry had propelled European (and American) military capability beyond the rest of the world, and they were more than willing to use force to solve any disputes that arose in the course of their seemingly never-ending expansion (Cao & Sun, 2011).

As Europe purchased tea, silk, and porcelain, silver flowed into the Qing Empire's only open port, Canton (now Guangzhou), but the Chinese in turn did not buy any European produce. A trade imbalance grew up, and the British hatched a plan to combat it; they would grow opium in their Indian provinces and turn a blind eye to traders dealing it to China.

The plan worked, and the practice of opium smoking spread throughout the interior of China and across all social classes. Silver, used by the Chinese to purchase opium, began to flow back into British coffers. For those involved in the supply, it was a very profitable enterprise; indeed, when addicted to opium, a life of languor and ruin beckoned. By 1839 CE, the Qing government had seen enough of the detrimental social effects to seize all of the opium found at the port of Guangzhou and throw it into the sea (Cao & Sun, 2011).

In response, the British launched a punitive mission. As George Macartney predicted 40 years prior, the Qing navy proved inadequate against British warships, which now included the ironclad and steam-powered H.M.S. *Nemesis* and the Qing capitulated as Britain seized territory across the south of China. By 1840 CE, Emperor Daoguang was forced to sign the *Treaty of Nanking*, at that point the most humiliating document ever signed by a Chinese Emperor. This document stipulated that a new joint Qing-British tariff system would be introduced and four more ports—Shanghai, Xiamen, Fuzhou, and Ningbo—would be opened to international trade. The island of Hong Kong was leased indefinitely to the British and British subjects in China (and everyone in Hong Kong) could now only be tried for crimes under British law, rather than Chinese law. Britain was also afforded a special status, whereby any future concessions extended to foreign nations would also be extended to Britain. Last but not least, to compensate Britain for the loss of opium in 1839 CE and for the expenses of the war, the Qing government would pay 21 million ounces of silver (Wright, 2011).

As one-sided as it was, the Treaty of Nanking was to be only the first of several declarations signed by the Qing known to the Chinese as the "Unequal Treaties". Opium continued to pour in through the newly opened ports, adding fuel to civil unrest that had been growing since the death of the Qianlong Emperor. In 1851 CE, the instability exploded into a conflict that rapidly spread across China. Hong Xiuquan, a man from the Hakka clan of ethnic Han who lived in southern China, declared himself Heavenly King of the Heavenly Kingdom of Peace. Hong had been influenced by Christian missionaries, and his syncretic vision was of a new China where the evils of Manchu rule and Confucian teachings had been overthrown. With its economy in tatters, its national pride stung by defeat to the British, and the Qing government unable or unwilling to respond to food shortages and the breakdown of law and order, Hong's message found many followers amongst the urban poor (Cao & Sun, 2011).

In one of the lesser-known conflicts of world history, the Qing Empire devolved into a state of civil war. It was an exceedingly bloody war, in which the combatants were equipped with modern weaponry attained through the treaty ports. By 1853 CE, Hong's forces had seized Nanjing and declared it the capital of his new kingdom. Sensing weakness, foreign powers circled like vultures around the ailing Empire. In 1856 CE, the British used a minor incident to incite a full-scale war, beginning the Second Opium War. The Americans and the French joined the British, and by 1860 CE, Beijing had been captured, and the Emperor's Summer Palace burnt to the ground. As with the First Opium War, a defeated China was forced to sign an onerous treaty, ceding yet more of its territory to foreign powers. With this treaty, the

British achieved their initial objective of legalizing the opium trade, and at the same time, they legalized the ability of foreign powers to export Chinese citizens as workers—they had managed to turn the people of China into yet another commodity to be exploited, yet more grist for the colonial mill.

The 200-year-old Qing Dynasty was reeling. With the need for modernization along the lines of the Western powers obvious, ambitious officials and generals who undertook a program of studying and adopting western science, technology, and industry formed the Self-Strengthening Movement. Parallel to this development, a five-year-old Emperor, Emperor Tongzhi, was enthroned and his mother, Empress Dowager Cixi, took hold of the reins of imperial power. In a period known as the Tongzhi restoration, Cixi backed the Self-Strengthening Movement ahead of other court factions, and Qing China began to rebuild. In

1871 CE, the Taiping Rebellion was finally put down, due in part to the modernized military capability of the Self-Strengthened Qing (Keay, 2009).

Unfortunately, Qing China was still suffering. The Taiping Rebellion had devastated the land, and the legalized opium trade now saw society burdened by millions of users and addicts. Meanwhile, tensions were rising in the Korean peninsula, historically a loyal tributary of the Qing. When war broke out with Japan in 1894 CE, the Qing were facing another modernizing Asian state. While the Tongzhi restoration aimed for a modernized military to protect the Empire and its ancient social order, the contemporary Meiji restoration of Japan had seen Japan transform completely in imitation of the European powers, with a constitutional monarchy, education-for-all, and a fully functional industrial base. Partially modern China proved no match for fully modern Japan, and in less than a year the war was over, with Taiwan ceded to the Japanese (Wright, 2011).

Whereas defeat by the British was at least mitigated by their mysterious origins and obviously superior technology, defeat to a member of the East Asian geopolitical order that the Chinese perceived as historically lesser was a devastating blow to the collective Chinese psyche. In response, in 1898 CE, Emperor Guangzhou instituted a series of reforms aimed at modernizing China as fully as the Meiji restoration had modernized Japan. The reform movement lasted for little more than 103 days before Empress Dowager Cixi backed conservative members of the court and had the Emperor, her nephew, jailed under house arrest (Cao & Sun, 2011).

Amongst the common people, anti-foreign sentiment surged, culminating in the Boxer

Rebellion of 1899 CE. The Boxers, named by the Europeans because they practiced martial arts similar to western "boxing", were groups of largely unemployed youth who began to band together to attack what they saw as foreign influences poisoning China; most often Christian missionaries or Chinese converts (Keay, 2009). In 1900 CE, Cixi issued a proclamation in support of the Boxers and their mission to eliminate China of foreign influence, and the movement spread like wildfire. Churches were burned, Christians were massacred, and the diplomatic quarter of Beijing came under siege.

Eventually, a multi-national force was able to liberate the consulates and to occupy the north of China as Cixi and her court, disguised as peasants, fled inland. In the aftermath, the Boxer Protocol was signed in 1901 CE, ceding yet more control of Chinese territory to the assembled interests of Europe, Russia, and

Japan, and burdening the Qing treasury with yet more exorbitant war reparations.

A chastened Cixi returned to the capital in 1902 CE, promising social reforms that were never fully realized. She died on November 15, 1908 CE, one day after enthroning her two-year-old grand-nephew as the Xuantong Emperor, and one day after his uncle, the Guangxu Emperor, still under house arrest, had been poisoned to death with arsenic (Kerr, 2013).

# CHAPTER 9
# *REVOLUTION AND WORLD WAR*

---

One of the turning points of 20th-century Chinese history took place in London, England:

*Sun Yat-Sen handed the housekeeper his laundry. At least during this captivity, they had allowed him some small courtesies. Given that they had already told him when and how he was going to be killed, it was most probably a pretense at civility—keeping up appearances in front of the non-Chinese staff, people like Mrs. Howe, the housekeeper.*

*Dr. Sun Yat-Sen was a prisoner inside the Chinese Legation in London, a small diplomatic fragment of the Qing Dynasty within the boundaries of the United Kingdom. The imperial secret service had kidnapped him, bundling him off of the street and into the premises. In a few days' time, he would be secreted onto a ship; returned to China to face show-trial and execution for his revolutionary activities.*

*His only hope was the note that he had left in his laundry, and his trust in Mrs. Howe's ability to get the message to Sir James Cantlie, his old friend and former medical school professor.*

Dr. Sun Yat-Sen, depending on who you asked, was either China's leading republican intellectual, or a dangerous enemy of the Qing Dynasty (Kerr, 2013).

## Sun Yat-Sen and the Revolution

The 19th century was a time of intellectual and political foment in the Western world. Reacting against the exploitation of workers and the domination of hereditary monarchs, nationalist and republican sentiments spread throughout western society. When Marx and Engels published their *Communist Manifesto* in 1858, it gave voice to the yearnings of downtrodden millions. At this time, China was still separated from the west by the barrier of language and culture, and the interior was still largely agrarian rather than industrial. Educated upper-class Chinese, however, and lower to middle-class Chinese involved in trading with foreigners, were able to gain access to the ideas pulsing through Europe, the Americas, and Russia in those times.

One such lower-class Chinese man was Sun Deming, known to history as Sun Yat Sen, an ethnic Han from Guangdong in southern China. Aged 12, he traveled to live in Honolulu, Hawaii, with his elder brother, who paid for his English education. In 1883, Sun returned to China and was further educated in Hong Kong as a western medical doctor. He also was baptized as a Christian at this time and became an active thinker at the head of one of the many republican groups that were growing in response to what they saw as the weakness and backwardness of the Qing Empire.

When China was defeated by Japan in the first Sino-Japanese war, Sun Yat-Sen's mind was made up—an overthrow of the monarchy and founding of a republican government was the only way forward for the nation. He was one of the leaders of a civil uprising in Guangzhou in 1895 that was soon quashed by Qing troops, and he fled into exile overseas (Wright, 2011).

While in exile, Sun continued to develop his thoughts and to correspond with leaders of the republican movement in China. It was during his exile that he was kidnapped by agents of the Qing, and only set free because he had managed to notify Sir James Cantlie of his predicament. Throughout his travels, he continually proselytized for his cause, finding most support from members of the overseas Chinese diaspora, especially those living in Southeast Asia. By 1911, he was the figurehead of a movement that threatened to sweep across China. In October 1911, his supporters initiated the Wuchang Uprising, announcing the new Chinese Republic. The Qing Empire sent General Yuan Shikai, a leader who had rebuilt the Qing army after the humiliation of the Sino-

Japanese conflict, to put down the uprising, but instead, the General decided to parlay with its leaders.

When General Yuan returned to Beijing, he had made a deal to replace Sun Yat-Sen as honorary President of the Republic of China. On February 12, 1912, Empress Dowager Longyu had no option but to sign the abdication letter on behalf of the six-year-old Xuantong Emperor. In doing so, two millennia of dynastic Chinese history had ended, and a new Republican era had begun (Cao & Sun, 2011). A democratic national assembly was formed, after which the first election was largely split between a republican faction that supported General Yuan and a coalition of nationalists supporting Sun Yat-Sen who renamed themselves the Kuomintang party (KMT). The Kuomintang, under their parliamentary leader Song Jiaoren, had become the most powerful party under the democratic arrangement—a state of affairs that the republicans were not willing to tolerate, in March 1913, Song Jiaoren was assassinated, most probably on the orders of Yuan Shikai.

The Kuomintang took up arms but were rapidly defeated by Yuan Shikai's superior forces, and Sun Yat-Sen fled overseas once again. The shining new republic had rapidly devolved into dictatorship. In 1915, when Japan presented its *21 Demands*, an aggressive attempt at subverting China within its sphere of influence, Yuan was able to repulse most of the Japanese ambitions with diplomatic support from the U.S. and Britain. His international standing is now more secure, on December 12, 1915, he declared himself the ruler of a new Empire of China (Kerr, 2013).

Emperor Yuan had badly misread public sentiment, and support for his government immediately began to disintegrate, with even former allies abandoning him. On March 22, 1916, He abdicated his new throne, and, with his health failing, died shortly afterward. China had entered the Warlord Period, as central control completely broke down and regional military governors began to carve up China between themselves (Wright, 2011).

## Chang Kai-Shek's China

In the wake of the collapse of Yuan Shikai's regime, the Kuomintang retreated to their heartland in the south. Sun Yat-Sen returned to Guangzhou and, in 1921, set up a military government. Bemoaning the fractured nature of China, Sun Yat-Sen made plans to unify the country by military conquest. His guiding principles of (i) nationalism, (ii) democracy, and (iii) welfare drew broad support from amongst the nationalist groups of China, and he made alliances in order to increase his power base. Most notably, he allied with the newly founded

Chinese Communist Party (CCP), enabling him to court alliance with Soviet Russia, then under the control of Vladimir Lenin (Wright, 2011).

One of the men he sent to study with the Russians was his trusted friend Chiang Kai-Shek, a young former soldier who had spent time serving in the Japanese army. Before Sun Yat-Sen could lead his alliance north to recapture the country from the warlords, he died of gallbladder cancer. After a brief power struggle, Chiang Kai-Shek assumed leadership of the KMT and, in 1926, he launched Sun's planned Northern Expedition.

During the expedition, tensions rose between Chiang Kai-Shek's faction and the CCP, and in 1927 he instigated a purge of the Chinese communists, massacring thousands, and instigating the Chinese Civil War. By 1928, the KMT had succeeded in capturing Beijing, and

China was once again unified. Chiang Kai-Shek then embarked upon a plan of modernization that was largely a success in the urban and industrial areas of the coastline. In the vast interior, however, rural life was little affected by these changes; with a steadily growing population—that had reached half a billion by 1930—and a static amount of arable land, hardship was, if anything, increasing (Kerr, 2013).

The KMT government lacked control of large areas of this poverty-stricken hinterland, its authority unrecognized either by the warlords, ethnic factions, or CCP guerillas. In September 1931, the weakness of this fragile "Republic of China" was laid bare to the world when the Japanese suddenly launched an invasion and annexation of Manchuria.

Despite this provocation, Chiang Kai-Shek did

not risk outright war with Japan and instead focused his attention on defeating the CCP. By 1933, his generals were able to completely surround the Communist-controlled highland area of Jiangxi province, encircling their perimeter with a series of connected fortifications. Calling in air support, Chiang Kai-Shek ordered complete annihilation of the trapped Communists (Wright, 2011).

# The Long March of the Communists

On May 4, 1919, a student uprising saw Tiananmen Square filled with protest. Society was changing in the wake of the dismissal of the Emperor, and a China-driven by "science" and governed by "democracy" were the demands of the youth (Cao & Sun, 2011). Only two years previously, a revolution had swept the neighboring state of Russia, promising a world without monarchs and capitalists.

A young man named Mao Zedong was a student in Beijing at this time, and like many of his compatriots, he was searching for answers that would lead to a better China, and a better world. He found these answers in the company of a group of intellectuals who, in July 1921, would find the Chinese Communist Party.

Mao first acted as a secretary for the Party during their time of alliance with the KMT, but this role would rapidly change when the KMT instituted their purges. Mao was appointed Commander-in-Chief of the militant wing of the CCP, the Red Army. After an assault on the city of Changsha failed, Mao and his forces retreated to the mountains of Jiangxi province where they would find their own communist state. Mao oversaw the seizure and redistribution of land from rich landowners and became highly popular with the impoverished peasant class (Wright, 2011).

By 1930, Mao's position was strong enough to attract the leadership of the CCP to join him, who then announced the formation of the "Soviet Republic of China"; an independent communist republic operating within the boundaries of nationalist China. Chiang Kai-Shek responded in 1931 with an encirclement campaign designed to isolate and destroy the communists. Using guerilla tactics, the CCP was at first able to hold off the nationalists, but by

1934, trapped in the center of a fortified ring via the encirclement campaign, the outlook for the "Soviet Republic of China" was bleak.

Spies within the KMT tipped off the CCP leadership that a coordinated land and air campaign was about to begin, and so the Red Army made a desperate attempt to break through the KMT lines. At high cost, 100,000 able-bodied members of the Red Army and CCP were able to escape southwest. Mao's plan was to evade the KMT by traversing the uplands of the interior of China, eventually joining forces with CCP allies in Shaanxi province. From northern China, Mao reasoned, they would be in a better position to liberate Manchuria from the Japanese, and thus, they would win the support of the Chinese public.

So began the Long March, a 370-day journey that took them west across the mountains of southern China, then north along the mountainous edge of the Tibetan plateau, then east across the plains to their destination of Shaanxi, nestled in the loop of the Yellow River. Pursued by KMT forces and their regional allies, exposed to disease and inclement weather, and altogether lacking in food supplies, the march took a devastating toll. Only 10% of those who broke out from the Jiangsu encirclement made it to their final destination, Yan'an (Kerr, 2013).

During the march, Mao's credentials had seen him move from deputy leader to leader of the Communist party with Zhao Enlai and Deng Xiaoping as his deputies. Once in Yan'an, he set about transforming rural society in the same way he had in Jiangxi, and his new power base began to grow (Wright, 2011). Before conflict with the KMT could resume, world events overtook both Mao Zedong and Chiang Kai-Shek.

## Japan Invades

Following a minor incident on July 7, 1937, between Chinese nationalist and Japanese soldiers outside of Beijing, the full might of the Japanese war machine was unleashed on China. The Second Sino-Japanese War, and the eastern theater of the Second World War, had begun.

The KMT and CCP signed a truce, theoretically joining forces against the Japanese aggressors. The major cities of Beijing, Shanghai, Nanjing, and, after fierce fighting, Wuhan, rapidly fell to the Japanese and the KMT, like the CCP before them, retreated far inland, moving their government to Chongqing on the Yangtze River. Red Army counterattacks against the Japanese invasion were highly successful, and their recruitment levels soared (Johnson, 1963). By 1940, hostilities between the KMT had resumed, as the CCP expanded the territory under their control and the KMT fought to contain them. The war against Japan had become a stalemate, but the balance began to tip in China's favor with the entrance of America into the conflict after the 1941 Japanese bombing of Pearl Harbor. Gradually, the Japanese were pushed back, before finally surrendering due to the atomic destruction of Hiroshima and Nagasaki (Wright, 2011).

## Civil War Resumes

At the end of World War II, the KMT and CCP were still allies on paper. Further peace talks between the two groups broke down, as the KMT was absolutely opposed to land seizure and redistribution, whereas the communists considered this policy non-negotiable. A 1946 military offensive by the KMT against the CCP was an initial success, but, by 1947, the CCP was able to retake lost ground. China's huge population of rural poor provided an unlimited recruiting pool for the CCP, and the Red Army continued to gain momentum. The Russian Soviet Army, which had occupied Manchuria in the wake of Japan's defeat, ceded it to the CCP, giving them overwhelming control of the north of China, and Mao's troops began to push their way south.

The KMT government was forced to retreat—first to Guangzhou, then Chengdu, until finally, in 1949, Chiang Kai-Shek and his supporters were airlifted to Taiwan. Chiang Kai-Shek's successors in the KMT are, as of 2021, still in control of Taiwan; hence the decades of tension between the CCP controlled mainland and the KMT controlled island.

On October 1, 1949, Mao gave a speech announcing victory in the Civil War from the Tiananmen Gate in Beijing. The People's Republic of China (PRC) was born (Kerr, 2013).

# CHAPTER 10
# *THE PEOPLE'S REPUBLIC OF CHINA*

———•••———

Chinese civil life would experience unprecedented change under communist rule:

*He heard them before he saw them. Their voices raised, their feet frantically pounding the paving stones. Puyi managed to get inside, slam and lock the door behind him. They were coming for him. He climbed the stairs, as fast as his frail, 60-year-old body would allow him, and surveyed the scene from a second-floor window.*

*There was a group of ten of them or so. Maybe 18 or 19 years old. Just kids. Whether male or female, they were all dressed the same—olive green army fatigues and olive-green caps. Their caps were emblazoned with a bright red star. It wasn't the words they were shouting that pained Puyi's heart, or the fact that they were flinging stones. It was the look on their faces. A fierce scowl that distorted the natural beauty of the young. A look of pure hatred.*

*Why was this gang of students harassing an elderly, bespectacled librarian? Because of what he stood for. They were Chairman Mao's Red Guards, and he was better known as Xuantong, the Last Emperor of the Qing Dynasty.*

As symbolic as it was, this episode was simply one among many—in 1966, all across the country, elders were being harassed and abused by their juniors as China underwent the tumult of Mao's *Cultural Revolution* (Szczepanski, 2019).

# Taking The Great Leap Forward

Their control of mainland China assured Mao and the Communist Party began transforming China in their own image. In an echo of the purges that the Communists faced under Chiang Kai-Shek, urban political enemies of the CCP were hunted down, interrogated, and tried. In the countryside, the CCP policy of land seizure and redistribution was extended nationwide. Mao ensured that the peasants themselves, rather than the army, would be involved in delivering the beatings and executions of the landlords; in this way, they became integral actors in the process of the revolution (Kerr,

2013).

Crisis intervened in 1950 when North Korea, then a Soviet Russian protectorate, invaded South Korea, a United Nations protectorate. The United Nations, led by the U.S., staged a counter-invasion that drove the North Korean forces back, mere miles from the border with China. It was at this stage that the Chinese, fearing the arrival of U.S. troops on Chinese soil, intervened, pouring over one million troops into the conflict. The United Nations force was repelled, pushed back to the 38th parallel, the original line of demarcation of the divided country, and an armistice was signed (Wright, 2011).

Bolstered by this surprising success against their natural enemies, imperialist capitalists, the Communist Party was ready to begin its next stage of social transformation. The U.S. and its allies had been angered by the intervention, and a trade embargo confirmed the PRC's status as an international pariah. On the other hand, their relationship with Soviet Russia was stronger than ever, and it was to their Communist brothers that the CCP leadership turned to aid them in the development and execution of their first Five Year Plan. Beginning in 1953, China mass-mobilized its population with the aim of developing a base of heavy industry. In concert with this industrial program, the joining together of farms as collective enterprises was encouraged.

It was a time of great promise for the rural poor, who for the first time in history were given access to free schooling, free healthcare, and even free meals. The demands of collective enterprise also necessitated improved literacy and the development of new skills. This period of the 1950s could be called "Mao's Golden Age"—it even included a brief period of political openness in 1956 called "The Hundred Flowers Campaign" where people were mandated to criticize mistakes made by the Communist Government in writing (Keay, 2009).

By 1957, the perhaps too-criticized Mao had reneged on the spirit of openness; using the evidence provided by the recorded criticisms, he mercilessly purged opponents of the CCP from society. Maoism had taken a greater grip on life in China, and he now forged ahead with his Second Five Year Plan. This was not to be a plan on the Russian model, this was to be an indigenously developed plan to make use of China's greatest resource: its prodigious supply of rural labor.

The farming collectives across China were merged into even larger units known as communes. These communes were both agricultural and industrial. Every commune built at least one kiln in which to process metals. With hundreds of thousands of kilns in place throughout the vast country, surely it would be a simple task to achieve Mao's goal of equaling Britain's steel output (Wright, 2011). As it happened, the primitive kilns with their inadequate material inputs could not even produce steel, let alone match the output of any major industrial nation. As disappointing as this must have been for the CCP leadership, of far more concern was the effect the policies were having on agricultural production. In the fervor to achieve the stated objectives of the Second Five Year Plan, records were being falsified and yields were being over-reported at all levels; from the farm laborer to the high administrators. The grain that did actually enter the communal granaries was then prioritized in its distribution to the cities, rather than to the villagers who had grown it, with some even being sent overseas to pay off debts (Keay, 2009).

The upper leadership of the CCP was either not willing or not able to believe the catastrophe unfolding on their doorstep, and late 1950s and early 1960's China—with food restrictions exacerbated by a flooding Yellow River and countrywide pest outbreaks—was a time of massive famine. One Communist Party member dispatched to the provinces described dead bodies piled up in every village he visited. These bodies were half-eaten. When he questioned the villagers on what had happened to the dead, they answered that the dogs had been eating them. He knew this to be a lie because the dogs themselves had all been eaten many months before (Jisheng, 2012).

It was a tragedy that took the lives of untold tens of millions, most likely the worst famine in human history, and altogether the setback was one that not even a near-deified leader like Mao could ride out. Tensions with Soviet Russia had also risen, with the Chinese disappointed by what they saw as a movement away from Marxism in the wake of Stalin's death, while the Russians for their part were aghast at Mao's cavalier attitude to the dangers of nuclear conflict:

> *"China has many people. They cannot be bombed out of existence ...*
>
> *The deaths of 10 or 20 million people are nothing to be afraid of."*
>
> - Mao Zedong (quoted in Li, 1994)

Mao resigned as Chairman of the People's Republic of China and retreated from frontline politics, while still remaining the paramount leader of the country as head of the military and Chairman of the Communist Party (Keay, 2009).

## The Cultural Revolution

Now adrift in the international wilderness, China took a more pragmatic turn as two other veterans of the Long March assumed frontline leadership: Zhou Enlai and Deng Xiaoping. Zhou was a longtime supporter of Mao, but a moderating influence both on Mao and other members of the party, while Deng was a realist, who valued results on the ground over political theorizing. Deng's philosophy could be summarized by an old Chinese parable that he was fond of quoting: "it doesn't matter if the cat is black or white, if it catches mice, it is a good cat" (MacFarquhar & Schoenhals, 2008). Grain was imported to help ease the famine, the collectives were disbanded, and small-scale market activity was allowed to resume. Slowly, China began to recover (Wright, 2011).

This liberalizing influence, however, was not

going to last. In 1966, Mao returned from his period of introspection, determined to re-stamp his authority on the party and on China. To Mao, those who had appropriated leadership of the Communist Party from him were nothing less than a new bourgeoisie rising up to dominate the proletariat; "capitalist roaders," putting China on course to follow what he saw as Russian Soviet capitulation to the West. According to Mao, what was needed was for the younger generations to experience a return to the origins of the revolutionary struggle (Keay, 2009).

To this end, he called for "The Great Proletarian Cultural Revolution". A working committee composed of his most dedicated followers was set up to guide the movement, and a sycophantic general, Lin Biao, was promoted to the twin positions of Vice Chairman of the Communist Party of China and Vice President of the People's Republic of China. It was Lin Biao who had compiled and published the famed *Little Red Book* of Mao's sayings that would go on to play such a central role in the upcoming upheaval (Wright, 2011).

Mao began to publicly censure his opponents in the Communist Party as his supporters became active amongst student groups across China. Mao lauded these student groups, proclaiming them his "Red Guards" and a tinderbox was lit across China. By August 1966, mass rallies were being held in Beijing, where Mao appeared in front of millions of red-clad students who brandished his *Little Red Book* aloft while fervently chanting revolutionary slogans. Mao told them that proletarian authority in China was being usurped by "intellectuals and counter-revolutionaries," in schools, universities, and even the Communist Party itself. Rebellion against these forces was therefore justified under Mao's rhetoric.

The mass hysteria grew, and gangs of Red Guards spontaneously sprang up across the whole country, attacking everything that spoke to them of China's history, bourgeois rule, or counter-revolution. Ancient temples were vandalized, priceless heirlooms smashed, and precious artwork destroyed. Far more distressing, lives were also destroyed—across China, teachers were pulled from their classrooms, doctors from their surgeries, officials from their posts. The fanatical Red Guards then proceeded to "re-educate" their victims; criticizing them, spitting on them, beating them, forcing them to admit to political thought crimes. The lucky were sent to labor in the fields with the peasants, the unlucky to the grave (Wright, 2011).

To foreign observers, it was an outbreak of collective madness. Realizing that he was losing control of the movement, Mao ordered the army to act. The Red Guards were rounded up and, in a bizarre twist of fate, sent to the countryside to join the people they had recently denounced in forced rural manual labor.

It was not until Mao's health began to fail in the mid-1970s that a thaw in the culture of mutual suspicion and paranoia appeared. By that time, Mao's former anointed successor, Lin Biao, had mysteriously died in a plane crash while attempting to flee China. Political power was now concentrated in the hands of Mao loyalists known as the "Gang of Four"—Mao's fourth wife, Jiang Qing, and her associates Zhang Chunqiao, Yao Wenyuan, and Wang Hongwen. The moderating influence of Zhou Enlai ended with his death in January 1976, and Mao followed soon after in September of that year.

Before he passed, Mao was able to install the

next paramount leader of China: a hardline Maoist known as Hua Guofeng (Keay, 2009). The "Gang of Four" meanwhile, began a purge of moderates, including that most progressive member of the party: Deng Xiaoping.

## An Era of Modernization

While Hua Guofeng was a Maoist, he was also a pragmatist; he saw the Gang of Four as dangerous radicals who were likely to challenge his leadership. Having gained the trust of the military in the weeks following Mao's death, he quickly made his move. On October 6, 1976, the Gang of Four were summoned to an emergency meeting where, much to their surprise, they were promptly arrested. In later televised show trials, the four were found guilty of instigating the Cultural Revolution and jailed for life (Wright, 2011).

Hua Guofeng then acted to rehabilitate Deng

Xiaoping and other moderates and modernizers within the party, and Chinese society exhaled a collective breath of relief. The chaos of the Cultural Revolution was assigned to the past, the blame pinned squarely on Lin Biao and the Gang of Four, and once again China began to rebuild. Deng Xiaoping counseled a return to the policies that had served him and his late ally Zhou Enlai so well pre-Cultural Revolution: the "Four Modernizations." That is, the modernization of agriculture, industry, defense, and technology (Keay, 2009).

The communes were dismantled, and in the countryside, small-scale markets were allowed to resume. Infrastructure was improved, and credit and energy supplies became more readily available. Steps were also made to combat ongoing exponential population growth—by 1976 CE, China had reached a population of 930 million—with an official (but in practice often unenforceable) one-child policy. Deng

Xiaoping, the canny political veteran, was the driving force behind these changes, and by 1980, he had replaced Hua Guofeng as the paramount leader of China (Wright, 2011).

Under Deng's leadership, Communist China embarked upon an unprecedented experiment with capitalism. Special Economic Zones (SEZs) were opened up along the coast, where local authorities were free to adjust laws and taxation to attract foreign investment and were encouraged to enter into partnerships with foreign enterprises. In 1984 CE, these four zones were followed by fourteen more, and soon after the majority of the eastern seaboard was open for business. To lessen the burden of numbers on the state and on the ecology of China, the one-child policy was tightened (Wright, 2011). In tandem with these changes, steps were made to rehabilitate China's international reputation.

The alliance with capitalism and a new level of international openness, however, did not extend to the practice of democracy. Even as it appeared to modernize in the eyes of the world, the Communist Party continued to increase its level of control of the population. When frustrated student protests broke out in 1989, chanting the same slogans of the days of Mao's 1919 youth, "science and democracy!" martial law was declared and the spirit and bodies of youths crushed under the wheels of tanks (Wright, 2011).

## China Transforms

The Tiananmen Square massacre shocked the world, and China almost found itself in the international wilderness once again. While the nations of the West protested, they did not fully cut ties with China. The tendrils of capitalism were now too deeply rooted; China and the west found themselves linked in an economic system of mutual dependence. It was now "the workshop of the world," and the international market was desperate for the products of that workshop (Kerr, 2013). The West may have placed an arms embargo on China, but they did not go so far as to liquidize their significant investments.

In the wake of the crackdown on democracy, the movement towards a more modern country stalled until 1992, when then retired Deng Xiaoping made a tour of southern China. On this tour of the SEZs, he publicly reiterated the importance of the economic reforms that he had begun in the late 1970s. Jiang Zemin, his successor at the head of the party, took heed of the elder statesman's counsel, and so began the next stage of the modernization of the Chinese economy (Zhao, 1993).

After 1992, the pace of economic liberalization

accelerated; state industries were privatized, tariffs and other barriers to international trade were reduced, and China became a member of the World Trade Organization. The SEZs were extended to the inland capitals of the major provinces, and to paraphrase Deng, getting rich was now considered to be glorious (Whiteley, 2007).

This hybrid socialist-capitalist system, or "Socialism with Chinese characteristics," pioneered by Deng Xiaoping, and continued by his successors, has transformed China in remarkable ways (Wright, 2011). In 1981, according to the World Bank, 90% of the population of China lived in absolute poverty, but by 2013, this figure was down to only 2%. The average citizen did not only move out of poverty during this time, they moved into prosperity, with per capita GDP growing by over 23 times in the period from 1978 to 2017 (qz.com).

From lacking basic infrastructure in 1978, China now leads the world in the construction of steel, ships, concrete, and textiles (Rawski, 2008). Even as the economy shifted away from agriculture, farmers still benefited from government support, with farming incredibly becoming exempt from taxation in 2005. Literacy now exceeds 97% of the population, and life expectancy has risen from only 40 years in 1940 to 76 years in 2019 (Kerr, 2013).

In 1997, Hong Kong was returned to China along with Macau in 1999 as China's international status burgeoned. Jiang Zemin's successor, Hu Jintao, adopted the "soft power" approach to international affairs, favoring openness, alliances, and investment over military coercion and economic threats. Hu Jintao's successor, Xi Jinping, built on the foundations of Hu Jintao's soft power era by beginning the construction of "Belt and Road Initiative", a series of foreign development partnerships that are building a 21st century equivalent of the ancient land and sea Silk Roads; connecting the markets and materials of both Eurasia and Africa together, with China as the lynchpin in the network (Morrison, 2019).

As of 2021, China is the world's second-biggest economy and is on course to overtake America in the next decade. It has the world's most valuable internet, mobile phone, and automobile markets and the world's largest holdings of foreign exchange reserves. In terms of manpower, its military is first in the world, only lagging behind the U.S. and Russia when the technological capability is accounted for. That technological gap is narrowing China is currently forging ahead with an ambitious manned space program, and has already sent unmanned vehicles to the Moon and Mars (nytimes.com).

Sitting at the center of the "Belt and Road", China is once more the Middle Kingdom; the crossroads and driving force of world trade and industry. Conditions are already in place to ensure that the 21st century will be China's century, but it remains to be seen what path the Chinese will take. As past imperial history has shown, negotiating the future is a delicate balancing act.

While progress has been made in health, wealth, and education, and the population stabilized, the unforeseen complication of a narrowing demographic pyramid has shrunk its labor pool, tax base, and disrupted its ratio of males to females. Thanks to the consequences of technology and heavy industry, the Chinese environment now suffers under a heavier burden than ever before (Kerr, 2013). While China has become a technological, industrial, and military leader, its political system remains resolutely undemocratic, with restrictions on information technology, the media, and free speech, under the auspices of a steadily developing surveillance state. Indeed, international concerns have been raised over the "vocational education and training centers" employed to contain and control ethnic Uyghurs in Xinjiang province (Canadian House of Commons, 2020).

China's rise to international pre-eminence was developed largely through "soft power", but under Xi Jinping, China has been more willing to use old-fashioned "hard power", as seen by its building of military bases in the South China Sea and its increased willingness to engage in border skirmishes. The future is not certain. In the globalized world of today, China's coming rise or fall will not just affect the Han people; it will affect us all.

# CONCLUSION

China's history is an incredible tale of inspiration, fortitude, ambition, chaos, and courage. Beginning from an era of myth and legend, archeological evidence reveals to us that it was one of the cradles of human civilization, developing independently from other comparable early civilizations such as the fertile crescent of the Middle East, the Indus Valley, or the western seaboard of Peru. Unlike these other civilizations of antiquity, Chinese culture—although undergoing cycles of rising, equilibrium, and collapse—continues to develop in response to internal and external pressures.

Our journey proceeded in five broad steps: reviewing the events, key personalities, and achievements of the five major eras of Chinese history:

### *Ancient China (pre-221 BCE)*

From the mists of time emerges the Shang writing system: the direct antecedent of the modern Chinese script and language. The Shang dynasty is where archeology draws the boundary of the recorded history of China, and Shang society is revealed to possess many of the core cultural qualities that we recognize today as "Chinese", such as pictographic writing, the manufacture of silk, the working of jade, and the religious veneration of ancestors (Keay, 2009).

Shang society progressed to Zhou society, and in

this feudal era, we saw the emergence of the classic philosophies of China, including Daoism and Confucianism. Civil and cultural life blossomed, but the authority of Zhou kingship was usurped as regional rulers began to war against one another.

## *The First Imperial Age (221 BCE to 580 CE)*

The first imperial age stretches from the unification of the warring states under the rulership of the Qin, through China's first "golden age" under the Han, to a long period of collapse and fragmentation that threatened to put an end to Chinese unity. This era saw the initial stages of what was to become The Great Wall, as well as the beginnings of the overland and maritime "Silk Roads" that would connect the economies of Europe and China, with some periods of interruption, to the present day.

## *The Second Imperial Age (581 CE to 1270 CE)*

The Second Imperial Age begins from the reunification of China under the Sui Dynasty, followed soon after by the establishment of the Tang Dynasty—China's second golden age; a time when the nation greatly expanded its borders and became enraptured of foreign influences, including the Indian religion of Buddhism, and the fruits of the trade from the Silk Road. China also exported its own high culture to Japan, Korea, and Vietnam during this era. After another period of near-collapse, China under the Song Dynasty prospered until enemies from the steppes took control.

## *The Third Imperial Age (1271 CE to 1911 CE)*

The rule of the Mongol Yuan marks the beginning of the third age of imperial history. As the Mongols were foreigners, their dynasty proved unpopular and was eventually overthrown by the native Han-led Ming. Under the Ming Dynasty, China demonstrated a seagoing potential capable of outstripping the burgeoning European Age of Discovery, but instead, the Chinese took an insular turn, halting their voyages of exploration. After a period of misgovernance and natural disaster, another tribe of foreigners seized the Empire—this was the Manchu-led Qing Dynasty, during which China once more experienced a period of great achievement and prosperity.

## *The Modern Age (1912 CE to present)*

The "Unequal Treaties" forced on the declining Qing Dynasty by Europe, the U.S., and Japan precipitated a crisis in the national consciousness of China, leading to the overthrow of the Empire and the establishment of a republic. This road to revolution was rocky and perilous, and fierce conflict between nationalists and communists was interrupted only by the Japanese invasion; an invasion that marked the onset of the eastern theater of World War II. After the war, and a final, bloody, struggle, the communists emerged victoriously. Their reign was to witness extreme crises, in the form of the *Great Chinese Famine* and the *Cultural Revolution*, before the nation rallied—undergoing a period of modernization and a resultant spectacular social, economic, and political rise.

Now that you have completed this journey, you have been informed of the mythology, the culture, the philosophy, the science, and the achievements of Chinese history. You are aware of great personages like Emperor Wu, Mao Zedong, Qin Shi Huangdi, and Confucius. You have witnessed how these and other luminaries, survived, failed, or prospered amid a variety of "interesting times". You have learned about the taming of mighty rivers and the digging of country-spanning canals, the development of extraordinarily productive agriculture, and treasure-bearing journeys across the oceans. You have been enlightened of thrilling court intrigues, secret societies preaching rebellion, and the depredations of the menacing tribes of the hinterlands and steppes.

You are now better equipped to understand the geography of China, the culture of the ethnic Han and the other ethnic groups that make up its population, China's recent history of intense civil conflict, and its recent emergence as a modern world superpower.

All of this is important because China's history is part of world history. Once upon a time, the course of the successive rise and fall of Chinese dynasties was remote and inaccessible to people in the western hemisphere. Now, Western economic destiny is interwoven with that of China—we buy clothes made in China, use electronics made in China, and travel in machines made in China. In turn, we sell the fruits of our own commerce, culture, and industry to China. The People's Republic of China is currently the majority holder of U.S. treasury bonds, and it has the largest military in the world. Its huge demand for energy and materials is bringing it into increasing conflict with other nations, with flashpoints in the South China Sea and the outer archipelagos of Japan, even as its leadership endeavors to negotiate peaceful international outcomes.

Are we witnessing the beginning of a new golden age for the Chinese, like that of the mighty Han or magnificent Tang? Or are we seeing signs of the beginning of an end—those times when the social fabric begins to fray as economic and ecological disasters overtake central control? China's future stability and prosperity will enable the future stability and prosperity of the entire world. China's collapse, on the other hand, would spell disaster for us all.

This was the history of China. This is **History Brought Alive**.

# PRONUNCIATION GUIDE

Chinese symbols representing whole words are commonly translated into a series of Roman characters according to a special pronunciation system. This pronunciation system is different from that used by an English speaker to read Roman characters.

Here are the major differences between English and Romanized Chinese (Pinyin):

| **Pinyin** | **Pronunciation Rule** |
|---|---|
| z | pronounced "dz" |
| Zh | pronounced "j" |
| Q | similar to "ch", but curling the tongue |

| | |
|---|---|
| X | similar to "sh", but curling the tongue |
| C | pronounced "ts" |
| Chi | the ending "i" is pronounced "err" |
| Shi | the ending "i" is pronounced "err" |
| Zhi | the ending "i" is pronounced "err" |

(Source: Upton-McLaughlin, 2013)

# TIMELINE

| Xia Dynasty | 2070–1600 BCE (unverified) |
|---|---|
| Shang Dynasty | 1600–1046 BCE |
| Western Zhou Dynasty | 1046–771 BCE |
| Spring and Autumn Period | 770–476 BCE |
| Warring States Period | 475–221 BCE |
| Qin Dynasty | 221–206 BCE |
| Western Han Dynasty | 206 BCE–8 CE |
| Eastern Han Dynasty | 25–220 CE |
| Three Kingdoms | 220–280 CE |
| Western Jin Dynasty | 226–316 CE |
| Eastern Jin Dynasty | 317–420 CE |
| Northern and Southern Dynasties | 420–589 CE |

| | |
|---|---|
| Sui Dynasty | 581–618 CE |
| Tang Dynasty | 618–907 CE |
| Five Dynasties and Ten Kingdoms | 907–960 CE |
| Northern Song Dynasty | 960–1127 CE |
| Southern Song Dynasty | 1127–1276 CE |
| Yuan Dynasty | 1271–1368 CE |
| Ming Dynasty | 1368–1644 CE |
| Qing Dynasty | 1636–1911 CE |
| Republic of China | 1912–1949 CE *continues in Taiwan |
| People's Republic of China | 1949–present |

(Source: Cao & Sun, 2011)

# END NOTE

If you have benefited from or enjoyed reading this concise and comprehensive journey through five millennia of China's history, please pass on those benefits and that enjoyment to others by leaving a review.

Thank you for your purchase. Don't forget to check out the rest of the cornucopia of myths, legends, and histories from around the world in the **History Brought Alive** series.

# REFERENCES

Beazley, C. R. (1903). The texts and versions of John de Plano Carpini and William de Rubruquis, as printed for the first time by Hakluyt in 1598, together with some shorter pieces (in Latin and English). London: Hakluyt Society.

Bergreen, L. (2007). Marco Polo: From Venice to Xanadu. Knopf.

Bo, Y. (1991). Complete Works. China Press.

Campbell, C. (2019). 'The Entire System Is Designed to Suppress Us.' What the Chinese Surveillance State Means for the Rest of the World. Time. URL: https://time.com/5735411/china-surveillance-privacy-issues/

Cao, D. & Sun. Y. (2011). China's History. Cengage Learning Asia Pte Ltd.

Chen, Y. J. (2018). Frontier, Fortification, and Forestation: Defensive Woodland on the Song-Liao Border in the Long Eleventh Century. Journal of Chinese History.

China Daily (2007). The Era of Prosperity is Upon Us. www.chinadaily.com.cn. URL: http://www.chinadaily.com.cn/opinion/2007-10/19/content_6243676.htm

Chinese script, Hangzhou. (2020). In www.unsplash.com. Retrieved December 9, 2021, from https://www.unsplash.com/photos/icVaVSd-8kQ

Chinese temple, Leshan. (2018). In www.pexels.com. Retrieved December 9, 2021, from https://www.pexels.com/photo/photography-of-the-temple-879359/

CIA (2021). China: The World Factbook. URL: https://www.cia.gov/the-world-factbook/countries/china/

Council on Foreign Relations. (2021). Territorial Disputes in the South China Sea. www.cfr.org. URL: https://www.cfr.org/global-conflict-tracker/conflict/territorial-disputes-south-china-sea

Dai, Y. & Gong, S. (2003). History of China: Illustrated Student Edition. Intelligence Press.

Ebrey, P. B. (2010). The Cambridge Illustrated History of China. Cambridge University Press.

Elverskog, J. (2010). Buddhism and Islam on the Silk Road. University of Pennsylvania Press.

Ferguson, J. C. & Masaharu, A. (1928). The Mythology of All Races: Volume VIII. Marshall Jones Company.

Finer, S. E. (1999) The History of Government from the Earliest Times: Volume III: Empires, Monarchies, and the Modern State. Oxford University Press.

Fowler, J. (2005). An Introduction to the Philosophy and Religion of Taoism: Pathways to Immortality. Brighton: Sussex Academic Press.

Gascoigne, B. & Gascoigne, C. (2003). The Dynasties of China. Perseus Books Group.

Gardner, D. K. (2014). Confucianism: A Very Short Introduction. Oxford.

Gill, B. & O'Hanlon, M. E. (1999). China's Hollow Military. Brookings. URL: https://www.brookings.edu/articles/chinas-hollow-military/

Great Wall, Jinshanling. (2020). In www.unsplash.com. Retrieved December 9, 2021, from https://www.unsplash.com/photos/E13mcj-2TLE

Jisheng, W. (2012). Tombstone: The Untold Story of Mao's Great Famine. Allen Lane.

Johnson, C. A. (1963). Peasant Nationalism and Communist Power: The Emergence of Revolutionary China, 1937-1945. The Journal of Politics.

Keay, J. (2009). China: A History. Basic Books.

Kerr, G. (2013). A Short History of China: From Ancient Dynasties to Economic Powerhouse. Pocket Essentials.

Kopf, D. & Lahiri, T. (2018). The astonishing impact of China's 1978 reforms, in charts. Quartz. URL: https://qz.com/1498654/the-astonishing-impact-of-chinas-1978-reforms-in-charts/

Li, Z. (1994). The Private Life of Chairman Mao. New York: Random House.

Longmen Grottoes. (2021). In www.pexels.com. Retrieved December 9, 2021, from https://www.pexels.com/photo/buddha

-statues-in-the-longmen-grottoes-8508726/

MacFarquhar, R. & Schoenhals, M. (2008). Mao's Last Revolution. Harvard University Press (2008).

Man, J. (2014). The Mongol Empire: Genghis Khan, His Heirs, and the Founding of Modern China. Bantam Press.

Mongol Falconer. (2018). In www.pexels.com. Retrieved December 9, 2021, from https://www.pexels.com/photo/cold-snow-fashion-man-6408355/

Morrison, W. M. (2019). China's Economic Rise: History, Trends, Challenges, and Implications for the United States. www.everycrsreport.com. URL: https://www.everycrsreport.com/reports/RL33534.html# Toc12530884

Myers, S. L. (2021). The Moon, Mars, and Beyond: China's Ambitious Plans in Space. The New York Times. URL: https://www.nytimes.com/article/china-mars-space.html

Perdue, P. C. (2005). China Marches West: The Qing Conquest of Central Eurasia. Belknap Press of Harvard University.

Peterson, B. B. (2000). Notable Women of China: Shang Dynasty to the Early Twentieth Century. Routledge.

Rawski, T. G. (2008). China's Great Transformation. Cambridge University Press.

Sima, Q. translated by Watson, B. (1993). Records of the Grand Historian. Columbia University Press.

Shanghai. (2017). In www.pexels.com. Retrieved December 9, 2021, from https://www.pexels.com/photo/landscape-photo-of-night-city-745243/

Spence, J. D. (2013). The Search for Modern China. W. W. Norton & Company.

Subcommittee on International Human Rights of the Canadian House of Commons Standing Committee on Foreign Affairs and International Development (2020). Statement by the Subcommittee on International Human Rights concerning the human rights situation of Uyghurs and other Turkic Muslims in Xinjiang, China.

Summer Palace, Beijing. (2020). In www.pexels.com. Retrieved December 9,

2021, from https://www.pexels.com/photo-of-a-palace-3960018/

Sussman, G. D. (2011). Was the Black Death in India and China? City University of New York Academic Works.

Szczepanski, K. (2019). Puyi, China's Last Emperor. ThoughtCo. URL: https://www.thoughtco.com/puyi-chinas-last-emperor-195612

Taagepera, R. (1997). Expansion and Contraction Patterns of Large Polities: Context for Russia. International Studies Quarterly. 41 (3): 492-502.

Talbot, M. (1991). The Holographic Universe. Harper Collins.

Temple of Heaven, Beijing. (2007). In www.pexels.com. Retrieved December 9, 2021, from https://www.pexels.com/photo/a-temple-under-the-blue-sky-5760659/

Terracotta Warriors, Xian. (2020). In www.unsplash.com. Retrieved December 9, 2021, from https://www.unsplash.com/photos/gUtcrNunbCM

Tiananmen Square, Beijing. (2020). In www.pexels.com. Retrieved December 9, 2021, from https://www.pexels.com/photo/people-walking-on-street-near-red-and-white-building-5075259/

Twitchett, D. (1998). The Cambridge History of China Volume 7 The Ming Dynasty 1368-1644, Part I. Cambridge University Press.

Upton-McLauchlin, S. (2013). A Guide to Hanyu Pinyin and Correct Chinese Pronunciation. The China Culture Corner. URL: https://chinaculturecorner.com/2013/09/22/pronouncing-chinese-pinyin/

Wilson Center. China's Soft Power Campaign. www.wilsoncenter.org. URL: https://www.wilsoncenter.org/chinas-soft-power-campaign/

Wright, D. C. (2011). The History of China. Greenwood.

Wu et al (2016). Outburst flood at 1920 BCE supports historicity of China's Great Flood and the Xia dynasty. Science. 353 (6299).

Zhang, Q. (2015). An Introduction to Chinese

History and Culture. Springer.

Zhao et al (2015). Ancient DNA Reveals That the Genetic Structure of the Northern Han Chinese Was Shaped Prior to three-thousand Years Ago. PLoS ONE.

Zhao, S. (1993). Deng Xiapoing's Southern Tour: Elite Politics in Post-Tiananmen China. Asian Survey. 33 (8) 739-756.

# OTHER BOOKS BY HISTORY BROUGHT ALIVE

- Ancient Egypt: Discover Fascinating History, Mythology, Gods, Goddesses, Pharaohs, Pyramids, and More from the Mysterious Ancient Egyptian Civilization.

Available now on Kindle, Paperback, Hardcover & Audio in all regions

- Greek Mythology: Explore The Timeless Tales Of Ancient Greece, The Myths, History & Legends of The Gods, Goddesses, Titans, Heroes, Monsters & More

Available now on Kindle, Paperback, Hardcover & Audio in all regions

- Mythology for Kids: Explore Timeless Tales, Characters, History, & Legendary Stories from Around the World. Norse, Celtic, Roman, Greek, Egypt & Many More

Available now on Kindle, Paperback, Hardcover

& Audio in all regions

- Mythology of Mesopotamia: Fascinating Insights, Myths, Stories & History From The World's Most Ancient Civilization. Sumerian, Akkadian, Babylonian, Persian, Assyrian and More

Available now on Kindle, Paperback, Hardcover & Audio in all regions

- Norse Magic & Runes: A Guide To The Magic, Rituals, Spells & Meanings of Norse Magick, Mythology & Reading The Elder Futhark Runes

Available now on Kindle, Paperback, Hardcover & Audio in all regions

- Norse Mythology, Vikings, Magic & Runes: Stories, Legends & Timeless Tales From Norse & Viking Folklore + A Guide To The Rituals, Spells & Meanings of Norse Magick & The Elder Futhark Runes. (3 books in 1)

Available now on Kindle, Paperback, Hardcover & Audio in all regions

- Norse Mythology: Captivating Stories & Timeless Tales Of Norse Folklore. The Myths, Sagas & Legends of The Gods, Immortals, Magical Creatures, Vikings &

More

Available now on Kindle, Paperback, Hardcover & Audio in all regions

- Norse Mythology for Kids: Legendary Stories, Quests & Timeless Tales from Norse Folklore. The Myths, Sagas & Epics of the Gods, Immortals, Magic Creatures, Vikings & More

Available now on Kindle, Paperback, Hardcover & Audio in all regions

- Roman Empire: Rise & The Fall. Explore The History, Mythology, Legends, Epic Battles & Lives Of The Emperors, Legions, Heroes, Gladiators & More

Available now on Kindle, Paperback, Hardcover & Audio in all regions

- The Vikings: Who Were The Vikings? Enter The Viking Age & Discover The Facts, Sagas, Norse Mythology, Legends, Battles & More

Available now on Kindle, Paperback, Hardcover & Audio in all regions

# FREE BONUS FROM HBA: EBOOK BUNDLE

Greetings!

First of all, thank you for reading our books. As fellow passionate readers of History and Mythology, we aim to create the very best books for our readers.

Now, we invite you to join our VIP list. As a welcome gift, we offer the History & Mythology Ebook Bundle below for free. Plus you can be the first to receive new books and exclusives!

Scan the QR code to join.

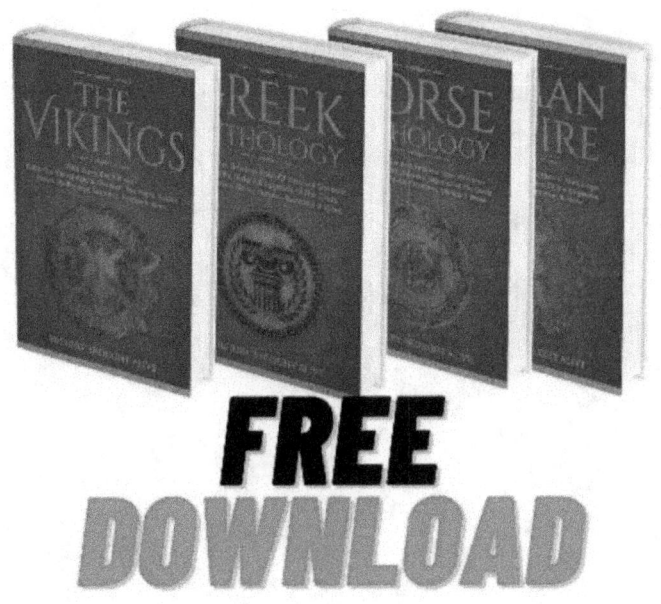

**Keep up to date with us on:**

YouTube: History Brought Alive

Facebook: History Brought Alive

www.historybroughtalive.com

www.ingramcontent.com/pod-product-compliance
Lightning Source LLC
Chambersburg PA
CBHW071613080526
44588CB00010B/1112